ABCs of Arabic & Islam

أَبْجَدِيات العَرَبِيّة والإسْلام

Sacred Strokes

Discovering the Beauty of the Qur'an through **Tracing**

Juz'
ʿAmma
Section
30th

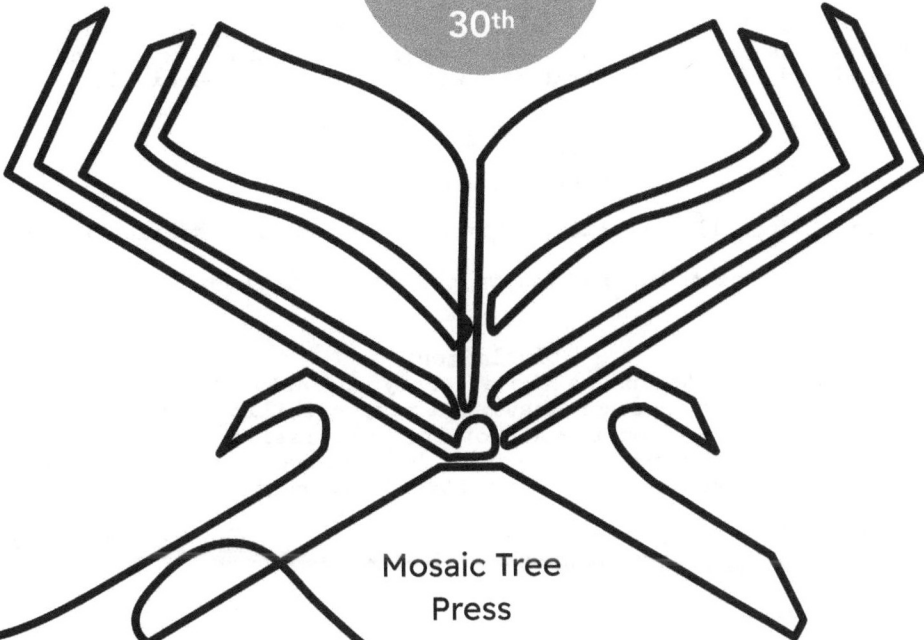

Mosaic Tree
Press

First published in 2025
by Mosaic Tree Press
www.MosaicTree.org

Book Design, Cover Illustration, Layout & Typesetting: Mosaic Tree Press

Printed and bound in the United Kingdom

Disclaimer:
Every effort has been made to ensure the accuracy and authenticity of the content in this book. The publisher and author assume no responsibility for errors, omissions, or the outcomes resulting from the use of the information contained herein. All names, examples, and references are used for educational purposes and do not imply endorsement unless stated otherwise.

To explore more titles by Mourad Diouri and discover resources for learners and educators, visit:
www.MosaicTree.org

Published by
Mosaic Tree Press

بسم الله الرحمن الرحيم

In the name of God, the Lord of Mercy, the Giver of Mercy

Contents

Tracing the Qur'an:
A Sacred Practice Rooted in Moroccan Tradition

In Morocco, Qur'anic education is not merely about memorising the sacred text — it is a deeply immersive, multi-sensory experience that draws on centuries of spiritual and pedagogical tradition. At the heart of this tradition lies the principle of **"At-tadrīb bi-l-kitābah (التَّدْريـب بـالـكِتابَـة)"** (learning through writing), where tracing and copying the Qur'an serve as powerful tools for internalising divine words. In traditional Qur'anic schools, known as Kuttāb (الـكُتّـاب) or Msīd (الـمُسـيد), children would sit in a semi-circle around the teacher M'allim (الـمُعَلِّم) or fqīh (الـفْقيه), each holding a wooden tablet Llūḥ (الـلّـوح) on which they would copy verses dictated to them. Using natural ink made from soot or herbs mixed with water and resin, they would carefully write, trace, and then read aloud what they had inscribed. The process was rhythmic and reverent — a blend of writing, reciting, listening, and visual focus. This method was not just instructional; it was formative, shaping the student's relationship with the Qur'an from a young age. The act of physically writing the Qur'anic script — letter by letter, word by word — was considered a spiritual exercise in discipline, presence ḥuḍūr (خُـضوـ), and respect. Students were often required to write and rewrite a verse several times before they were allowed to move on. Mistakes were corrected on the spot, and once the verse was memorised, the ink on the board would be washed away with water — a symbolic act of both cleansing and renewal. This traditional method embodies a holistic pedagogical approach:

- The hand internalises the shape and movement of the Arabic letters.
- The eye becomes familiar with Qur'anic orthography and structure.
- The ear tunes into rhythm and pronunciation through repetition and listening.
- The tongue refines articulation and Tajwīd through guided recitation.

Even today, in many rural and urban parts of Morocco, this method is still practised, especially in Zāwiyahs (زوايـا) (spiritual lodges) and Masājid-based learning circles. More recently, this heritage has inspired modern educational materials like tracing books, which aim to preserve the essence of traditional methods while making them accessible to new generations of learners, both in Morocco and beyond.

By reviving the practice of Qur'anic tracing, we honour this rich Moroccan tradition, allowing learners to engage with the Qur'an not just intellectually, but physically and spiritually, one sacred stroke at a time.

How to Trace the Qur'an Effectively

1. **Prepare Your Space and Intention (Niyyah نية):**
   - Sit in a quiet, respectful environment.
   - Begin with the **Basmalah (بسملة)**: *Bismillāhi-rraḥmānir-raḥīm*
   - Renew your intention: Tracing and reading the Qur'an is a form of worship (*ʿibādah* عبادة).

2. **Use a Clean Pen and Neat Handwriting:**
   - Pencil or fine tracing pen works best.
   - Aim for slow, deliberate movements.
   - Be mindful of dot placement, especially for similar-looking letters.

3. **Follow the Arabic Script Carefully:**
   - Always **trace from right to left**.
   - Observe the shapes of **joined letters** and spacing.
   - As you trace each verse, **repeat it aloud or whisper** it quietly.
   - Reflect on its meaning by reading the English translation, either as you go or once you've finished tracing.

4. **Work in Short Sections:**
   - Break down each verse (*āyah* آية) into small parts.
   - Repeat each part three times: **read, trace, recite**.

5. **After Tracing, Recite from Memory:**
   - Cover the script and try to recite what you've traced.
   - Visual recall of the writing will support memory retention.

6. **Daily Routine Tip:**
   - Trace 1–3 verses per day for consistent progress.
   - End your session with a short du'ā' (e.g., *Allāhumma yassir lī ḥifẓa kitābik* اللَّهُمَّ يَسِّرْ لِي حِفْظَ كِتَابِك).

Why Tracing Helps with Memorisation

Multi-Sensory Learning:

- Tracing engages the **eye, hand, mouth, and ear**, reinforcing long-term memory.

Focus and Slowness:

- Tracing slows the process of reading, helping the mind to absorb each word carefully.

Visual-Spatial Memory:

- Remembering how verses look on the page helps in **mental positioning** during recitation.

Writing as Worship:

- The act of writing the Qur'an is itself **rewarding and spiritually uplifting** — it encourages reflection and reverence.

Suitable for All Ages:

- Particularly effective for **young learners**, **visual learners**, and **beginner reciters**.

Reviving a Tradition

By tracing the Qur'an, you are reviving a **centuries-old Moroccan educational practice** that blends calligraphy, devotion, and memorisation. This method not only strengthens your connection with the sacred text but also honours the heritage of Qur'anic learners before you.

Note on Qur'an Translation

For consistency and clarity, all English renderings of Qur'anic verses in this book are taken from **Sahih International**, a widely respected contemporary translation. Known for its balance between accuracy and readability, Sahih International avoids unnecessary interpretive additions, while maintaining a simple and accessible style. This choice ensures that readers encounter a faithful yet approachable translation of the Qur'an throughout *Sacred Strokes*.

Note on the Qur'anic Arabic Text

All Qur'anic Arabic in this book is cited from the **Madinah Muṣḥaf (al-Muṣḥaf al-Madanī)**, the standardised edition printed by the King Fahd Complex in Madīnah. This text follows the **'Uthmānī script** and orthography, ensuring precision and consistency in reading, recitation, and study. Its widespread recognition makes it a reliable reference point for learners and readers alike.

Note on Arabic Phonetic Transliteration

The Arabic text is accompanied by a phonetic transliteration to guide accurate pronunciation for readers unfamiliar with Arabic script. This system uses diacritical markers such as ḥ, ', ā, ī, ū to represent Arabic sounds precisely, reflecting their classical pronunciation. The transliteration supports correct recitation, study, and memorisation, while remaining easy to read for learners at all levels.

Note on Verse Numbering (Hindi–Arabic Numbers)

All verse numbers follow the **Hindi–Arabic numeral system**, the traditional numbering used in Qur'anic manuscripts and printed Muṣḥafs. This system aligns with classical Qur'anic presentation and helps readers locate and reference verses consistently across different editions and study materials. The numbers correspond to the familiar Western/English numerals as follows: ٠ - 0, ١ - 1, ٢ - 2, ٣ - 3, ٤ - 4, ٥ - 5, ٦ - 6, ٧ - 7, ٨ - 8, ٩ - 9

Note on Juz' 'Amma

Juz' 'Amma refers to the **30th section of the Qur'an**, beginning with **Sūrat an-Naba'** **(78)** and ending with **Sūrat an-Nās (114)**. It contains the shortest and most frequently recited Sūrahs, making it especially accessible for beginners and widely used in memorisation. The Sūrahs focus on themes such as the **Hereafter, human accountability, divine signs, and moral guidance**, providing concise yet profound messages. This section is often the first part of the Qur'an taught to learners because of its brevity, rhythmic structure, and ease of recitation. In this book, *Sacred Strokes*, Juz' 'Amma is presented with **Arabic text, phonetic transliteration, and English translation** to support both study and correct pronunciation.

Trace each blessed letter of
Allah's Words carefully from right to left.
Take your time, focus on the meaning, and let
every stroke be an act of reflection.

Let's Begin

Bismillāh

بِسْمِ اللّٰه

In the Name of Allah

1. Say, "I seek refuge in the Lord of mankind,

2. The Sovereign of mankind,

3. The God of mankind,

4. From the evil of the retreating whisperer –

5. Who whispers in the breasts of mankind –

6. Among the jinn and mankind."

سورة الناس

Surāt An-Nās | Mankind [114]

بِسْمِ ٱللَّهِ ٱلرَّحْمَٰنِ ٱلرَّحِيمِ

قُلْ أَعُوذُ بِرَبِّ ٱلنَّاسِ ۝١ مَلِكِ ٱلنَّاسِ ۝٢ إِلَٰهِ ٱلنَّاسِ ۝٣ مِن شَرِّ ٱلْوَسْوَاسِ ٱلْخَنَّاسِ ۝٤ ٱلَّذِى يُوَسْوِسُ فِى صُدُورِ ٱلنَّاسِ ۝٥ مِنَ ٱلْجِنَّةِ وَٱلنَّاسِ ۝٦

1. Say, "I seek refuge in the Lord of daybreak

2. From the evil of that which He created

3. And from the evil of darkness when it settles

4. And from the evil of the blowers in knots

5. And from the evil of an envier when he envies.

سورة الفلق

Surāt Al-Falaq | The Daybreak / The Dawn [113]

بِسْمِ اللَّهِ الرَّحْمَٰنِ الرَّحِيمِ

قُلْ أَعُوذُ بِرَبِّ الْفَلَقِ ﴿١﴾ مِن شَرِّ مَا خَلَقَ ﴿٢﴾ وَمِن شَرِّ غَاسِقٍ إِذَا وَقَبَ ﴿٣﴾ وَمِن شَرِّ النَّفَّاثَاتِ فِي الْعُقَدِ ﴿٤﴾ وَمِن شَرِّ حَاسِدٍ إِذَا حَسَدَ ﴿٥﴾

1. Say, "He is Allah, [who is] One,

2. Allah, the Eternal Refuge.

3. He neither begets nor is born,

4. Nor is there to Him any equivalent."

سورة الإخلاص

Surāt Al-Ikhlāṣ | The Sincerity, The Purity of Faith [112]

بِسْمِ اللَّهِ الرَّحْمَٰنِ الرَّحِيمِ

قُلْ هُوَ اللَّهُ أَحَدٌ ۝ اللَّهُ الصَّمَدُ ۝ لَمْ يَلِدْ وَلَمْ يُولَدْ ۝

وَلَمْ يَكُن لَّهُ كُفُوًا أَحَدٌ ۝

1. May the hands of Abu Lahab be ruined, and ruined is he.

2. His wealth will not avail him or that which he gained.

3. He will [enter to] burn in a Fire of [blazing] flame

4. And his wife [as well] – the carrier of firewood.

5. Around her neck is a rope of [twisted] fiber.

سورة المسد

Surāt Al-Masad | The Palm Fiber, The Flame [111]

بِسْمِ اللَّهِ الرَّحْمَٰنِ الرَّحِيمِ

تَبَّتْ يَدَا أَبِي لَهَبٍ وَتَبَّ ﴿١﴾ مَا أَغْنَىٰ عَنْهُ مَالُهُ وَمَا كَسَبَ ﴿٢﴾

سَيَصْلَىٰ نَارًا ذَاتَ لَهَبٍ ﴿٣﴾ وَامْرَأَتُهُ حَمَّالَةَ الْحَطَبِ ﴿٤﴾

فِي جِيدِهَا حَبْلٌ مِّن مَّسَدٍ ﴿٥﴾

1. When the victory of Allah has come and the conquest,

2. And you see the people entering into the religion of Allah in multitudes,

3. Then exalt [Him] with praise of your Lord and ask forgiveness of Him. Indeed, He is ever Accepting of repentance.

سورة النصر

Surāt An-Naṣr | The Divine Support / The Help [110]

بِسْمِ ٱللَّهِ ٱلرَّحْمَٰنِ ٱلرَّحِيمِ

إِذَا جَآءَ نَصْرُ ٱللَّهِ وَٱلْفَتْحُ ۝ وَرَأَيْتَ ٱلنَّاسَ يَدْخُلُونَ فِي دِينِ ٱللَّهِ أَفْوَاجًا ۝ فَسَبِّحْ بِحَمْدِ رَبِّكَ وَٱسْتَغْفِرْهُ إِنَّهُ كَانَ تَوَّابًا ۝

1. Say, "O disbelievers,

2. I do not worship what you worship.

3. Nor are you worshippers of what I worship.

4. Nor will I be a worshipper of what you worship.

5. Nor will you be worshippers of what I worship.

6. For you is your religion, and for me is my religion.

سورة الكافرون

Surāt Al-Kāfirūn | The Disbelievers [109]

بِسۡمِ ٱللَّهِ ٱلرَّحۡمَٰنِ ٱلرَّحِيمِ

قُلۡ يَٰٓأَيُّهَا ٱلۡكَٰفِرُونَ ﴿١﴾ لَآ أَعۡبُدُ مَا تَعۡبُدُونَ ﴿٢﴾

وَلَآ أَنتُمۡ عَٰبِدُونَ مَآ أَعۡبُدُ ﴿٣﴾ وَلَآ أَنَا۠ عَابِدٌ مَّا عَبَدتُّمۡ ﴿٤﴾

وَلَآ أَنتُمۡ عَٰبِدُونَ مَآ أَعۡبُدُ ﴿٥﴾ لَكُمۡ دِينُكُمۡ وَلِيَ دِينِ ﴿٦﴾

1. Indeed, We have granted you, [O Muhammad], al-Kawthar.

2. So pray to your Lord and sacrifice [to Him alone].

3. Indeed, your enemy is the one cut off.

سورة الكوثر

Surāt Al-Kawthar | Abundance / The River of Plenty [108]

بِسْمِ ٱللَّهِ ٱلرَّحْمَٰنِ ٱلرَّحِيمِ

إِنَّآ أَعْطَيْنَٰكَ ٱلْكَوْثَرَ ۝١ فَصَلِّ لِرَبِّكَ وَٱنْحَرْ ۝٢

إِنَّ شَانِئَكَ هُوَ ٱلْأَبْتَرُ ۝٣

1. Have you seen the one who denies the Recompense?

2. For that is the one who drives away the orphan

3. And does not encourage the feeding of the poor.

4. So woe to those who pray

5. [But] who are heedless of their prayer –

6. Those who make show [of their deeds]

7. And withhold [simple] assistance.

سورة الماعون

Surāt Al-Māʿūn | Small Kindnesses / Assistance [107]

بِسۡمِ ٱللَّهِ ٱلرَّحۡمَٰنِ ٱلرَّحِيمِ

أَرَءَيۡتَ ٱلَّذِى يُكَذِّبُ بِٱلدِّينِ ۝١ فَذَٰلِكَ ٱلَّذِى يَدُعُّ ٱلۡيَتِيمَ ۝٢ وَلَا يَحُضُّ عَلَىٰ طَعَامِ ٱلۡمِسۡكِينِ ۝٣ فَوَيۡلٌ لِّلۡمُصَلِّينَ ۝٤ ٱلَّذِينَ هُمۡ عَن صَلَاتِهِمۡ سَاهُونَ ۝٥ ٱلَّذِينَ هُمۡ يُرَآءُونَ ۝٦ وَيَمۡنَعُونَ ٱلۡمَاعُونَ ۝٧

1. For the accustomed security of the Quraysh –

2. Their accustomed security [in] the caravan of winter and summer –

3. Let them worship the Lord of this House,

4. Who has fed them, [saving them] from hunger and made them safe, [saving them] from fear.

سورة قريش

Surāt Quraysh | Quraysh (The Tribe) [106]

بِسۡمِ ٱللَّهِ ٱلرَّحۡمَٰنِ ٱلرَّحِيمِ

لِإِيلَٰفِ قُرَيۡشٍ ﴿١﴾ إِۦلَٰفِهِمۡ رِحۡلَةَ ٱلشِّتَآءِ وَٱلصَّيۡفِ ﴿٢﴾ فَلۡيَعۡبُدُواْ رَبَّ هَٰذَا ٱلۡبَيۡتِ ﴿٣﴾ ٱلَّذِىٓ أَطۡعَمَهُم مِّن جُوعٍ وَءَامَنَهُم مِّنۡ خَوۡفِۭ ﴿٤﴾

1. Have you not considered, [O Muhammad], how your Lord dealt with the companions of the elephant?

2. Did He not make their plan into misguidance?

3. And He sent against them birds in flocks,

4. Striking them with stones of hard clay,

5. And made them like eaten straw.

سورة الفيل

Surāt Al-Fīl | The Elephant [105]

بِسْمِ اللَّهِ الرَّحْمَٰنِ الرَّحِيمِ

أَلَمْ تَرَ كَيْفَ فَعَلَ رَبُّكَ بِأَصْحَٰبِ الْفِيلِ ۝ أَلَمْ يَجْعَلْ

كَيْدَهُمْ فِي تَضْلِيلٍ ۝ وَأَرْسَلَ عَلَيْهِمْ طَيْرًا أَبَابِيلَ ۝

تَرْمِيهِم بِحِجَارَةٍ مِّن سِجِّيلٍ ۝ فَجَعَلَهُمْ كَعَصْفٍ مَّأْكُولٍ ۝

1. Woe to every scorner and mocker

2. Who collects wealth and [continuously] counts it.

3. He thinks that his wealth will make him immortal.

4. No! He will surely be thrown into the Crusher.

5. And what can make you know what is the Crusher?

6. It is the fire of Allah, [eternally] fuelled,

7. Which mounts directed at the hearts.

8. Indeed, Hellfire will be closed down upon them

9. In extended columns.

سورة الهمزة

Surāt Al-Humazah | The Slanderer [104]

بِسْمِ اللَّهِ الرَّحْمَٰنِ الرَّحِيمِ

وَيْلٌ لِّكُلِّ هُمَزَةٍ لُّمَزَةٍ ۝١ ٱلَّذِي جَمَعَ مَالًا وَعَدَّدَهُ ۝٢

يَحْسَبُ أَنَّ مَالَهُ أَخْلَدَهُ ۝٣ كَلَّا ۖ لَيُنْبَذَنَّ فِي ٱلْحُطَمَةِ ۝٤

وَمَا أَدْرَاكَ مَا ٱلْحُطَمَةُ ۝٥ نَارُ ٱللَّهِ ٱلْمُوقَدَةُ ۝٦ ٱلَّتِي تَطَّلِعُ

عَلَى ٱلْأَفْئِدَةِ ۝٧ إِنَّهَا عَلَيْهِم مُّؤْصَدَةٌ ۝٨ فِي عَمَدٍ مُّمَدَّدَةٍ ۝٩

1. By time,

2. Indeed, mankind is in loss,

3. Except for those who have believed and done righteous deeds and advised each other to truth and advised each other to patience.

سورة العصر

Surāt Al-'Aṣr | Time / The Declining Day [103]

بِسْمِ ٱللَّهِ ٱلرَّحْمَٰنِ ٱلرَّحِيمِ

وَٱلْعَصْرِ ﴿١﴾ إِنَّ ٱلْإِنسَٰنَ لَفِى خُسْرٍ ﴿٢﴾ إِلَّا ٱلَّذِينَ ءَامَنُوا۟ وَعَمِلُوا۟ ٱلصَّٰلِحَٰتِ وَتَوَاصَوْا۟ بِٱلْحَقِّ وَتَوَاصَوْا۟ بِٱلصَّبْرِ ﴿٣﴾

1. Competition in [worldly] increase diverts you

2. Until you visit the graveyards.

3. No! You are going to know.

4. Then no! You are going to know.

5. No! If you only knew with knowledge of certainty…

6. You will surely see the Hellfire.

7. Then you will surely see it with the eye of certainty.

8. Then you will surely be asked that Day about pleasure.

سورة التكاثر

Surāt At-Takāthur | The Piling Up / Competition [102]

بِسْمِ ٱللَّهِ ٱلرَّحْمَٰنِ ٱلرَّحِيمِ

أَلْهَىٰكُمُ ٱلتَّكَاثُرُ ﴿١﴾ حَتَّىٰ زُرْتُمُ ٱلْمَقَابِرَ ﴿٢﴾ كَلَّا سَوْفَ تَعْلَمُونَ ﴿٣﴾ ثُمَّ

كَلَّا سَوْفَ تَعْلَمُونَ ﴿٤﴾ كَلَّا لَوْ تَعْلَمُونَ عِلْمَ ٱلْيَقِينِ ﴿٥﴾ لَتَرَوُنَّ ٱلْجَحِيمَ ﴿٦﴾

ثُمَّ لَتَرَوُنَّهَا عَيْنَ ٱلْيَقِينِ ﴿٧﴾ ثُمَّ لَتُسْأَلُنَّ يَوْمَئِذٍ عَنِ ٱلنَّعِيمِ ﴿٨﴾

1. The Striking Calamity –

2. What is the Striking Calamity?

3. And what can make you know what is the Striking Calamity?

4. It is the Day when people will be like moths, dispersed,

5. And the mountains will be like wool, fluffed up.

6. Then as for one whose scales are heavy [with good deeds],

7. He will be in a pleasant life.

8. But as for one whose scales are light,

9. His refuge will be an abyss.

10. And what can make you know what that is?

11. It is a Fire, intensely hot.

سورة القارعة

Surāt Al-Qāri'ah | The Striking Calamity [101]

بِسْمِ اللَّهِ الرَّحْمَٰنِ الرَّحِيمِ

ٱلْقَارِعَةُ ﴿١﴾ مَا ٱلْقَارِعَةُ ﴿٢﴾ وَمَآ أَدْرَىٰكَ مَا ٱلْقَارِعَةُ ﴿٣﴾ يَوْمَ يَكُونُ ٱلنَّاسُ كَٱلْفَرَاشِ ٱلْمَبْثُوثِ ﴿٤﴾ وَتَكُونُ ٱلْجِبَالُ كَٱلْعِهْنِ ٱلْمَنفُوشِ ﴿٥﴾ فَأَمَّا مَن ثَقُلَتْ مَوَٰزِينُهُۥ ﴿٦﴾ فَهُوَ فِى عِيشَةٍ رَّاضِيَةٍ ﴿٧﴾ وَأَمَّا مَنْ خَفَّتْ مَوَٰزِينُهُۥ ﴿٨﴾ فَأُمُّهُۥ هَاوِيَةٌ ﴿٩﴾ وَمَآ أَدْرَىٰكَ مَا هِيَهْ ﴿١٠﴾ نَارٌ حَامِيَةٌۢ ﴿١١﴾

1. By the racers, panting,

2. And the producers of sparks [when] striking,

3. And the chargers at dawn,

4. Stirring up thereby [clouds of] dust,

5. Arriving thereby in the centre collectively,

6. Indeed mankind, to his Lord, is ungrateful.

7. And indeed, he is to that a witness.

8. And indeed he is, in love of wealth, intense.

9. But does he not know that when the contents of the graves are scattered

10. And that within the breasts is obtained,

11. Indeed, their Lord, that Day, is [fully] acquainted with them.

سورة العاديات

Surat Al-'Ādiyāt | The Courser / The Racers [100]

بِسْمِ اللَّهِ الرَّحْمَٰنِ الرَّحِيمِ

وَالْعَادِيَاتِ ضَبْحًا ﴿١﴾ فَالْمُورِيَاتِ قَدْحًا ﴿٢﴾ فَالْمُغِيرَاتِ صُبْحًا ﴿٣﴾ فَأَثَرْنَ بِهِ نَقْعًا ﴿٤﴾ فَوَسَطْنَ بِهِ جَمْعًا ﴿٥﴾ إِنَّ الْإِنسَانَ لِرَبِّهِ لَكَنُودٌ ﴿٦﴾ وَإِنَّهُ عَلَىٰ ذَٰلِكَ لَشَهِيدٌ ﴿٧﴾ وَإِنَّهُ لِحُبِّ الْخَيْرِ لَشَدِيدٌ ﴿٨﴾ ۞ أَفَلَا يَعْلَمُ إِذَا بُعْثِرَ مَا فِي الْقُبُورِ ﴿٩﴾ وَحُصِّلَ مَا فِي الصُّدُورِ ﴿١٠﴾ إِنَّ رَبَّهُم بِهِمْ يَوْمَئِذٍ لَّخَبِيرٌ ﴿١١﴾

1. When the earth is shaken with its [final] earthquake

2. And the earth discharges its burdens

3. And man says, "What is [wrong] with it?" –

4. That Day, it will report its news

5. Because your Lord has commanded it.

6. That Day, the people will depart separated [into categories] to be shown [the result of] their deeds.

7. So whoever does an atom's weight of good will see it,

8. And whoever does an atom's weight of evil will see it

سورة الزلزلة

Surāt Az-Zalzalah | The Earthquake [99]

بِسْمِ ٱللَّهِ ٱلرَّحْمَٰنِ ٱلرَّحِيمِ

إِذَا زُلْزِلَتِ ٱلْأَرْضُ زِلْزَالَهَا ﴿١﴾ وَأَخْرَجَتِ ٱلْأَرْضُ أَثْقَالَهَا ﴿٢﴾ وَقَالَ ٱلْإِنسَٰنُ مَا لَهَا ﴿٣﴾ يَوْمَئِذٍ تُحَدِّثُ أَخْبَارَهَا ﴿٤﴾ بِأَنَّ رَبَّكَ أَوْحَىٰ لَهَا ﴿٥﴾ يَوْمَئِذٍ يَصْدُرُ ٱلنَّاسُ أَشْتَاتًا لِّيُرَوْا۟ أَعْمَٰلَهُمْ ﴿٦﴾ فَمَن يَعْمَلْ مِثْقَالَ ذَرَّةٍ خَيْرًا يَرَهُۥ ﴿٧﴾ وَمَن يَعْمَلْ مِثْقَالَ ذَرَّةٍ شَرًّا يَرَهُۥ ﴿٨﴾

1. Those who disbelieved among the People of the Scripture and the polytheists were not to be parted [from misbelief] until there came to them clear evidence –

2. A Messenger from Allah, reciting purified scriptures

3. Within which are correct writings.

4. Nor did those who were given the Scripture become divided until after there had come to them clear evidence.

5. And they were not commanded except to worship Allah, [being] sincere to Him in religion, inclining to truth, and to establish prayer and to give zakah. And that is the correct religion.

6. Indeed, they who disbelieved among the People of the Scripture and the polytheists will be in the fire of Hell, abiding eternally therein. Those are the worst of creatures.

7. Indeed, those who have believed and done righteous deeds – those are the best of creatures.

8. Their reward with their Lord will be gardens of perpetual residence beneath which rivers flow, wherein they will abide forever, Allah being pleased with them and they with Him. That is for whoever has feared his Lord.

سورة البينة

Surāt Al-Bayyinah | The Clear Proof [98]

بِسۡمِ ٱللَّهِ ٱلرَّحۡمَٰنِ ٱلرَّحِيمِ

لَمۡ يَكُنِ ٱلَّذِينَ كَفَرُواْ مِنۡ أَهۡلِ ٱلۡكِتَٰبِ وَٱلۡمُشۡرِكِينَ مُنفَكِّينَ حَتَّىٰ

تَأۡتِيَهُمُ ٱلۡبَيِّنَةُ ۝ رَسُولٞ مِّنَ ٱللَّهِ يَتۡلُواْ صُحُفٗا مُّطَهَّرَةٗ ۝ فِيهَا كُتُبٞ

قَيِّمَةٞ ۝ وَمَا تَفَرَّقَ ٱلَّذِينَ أُوتُواْ ٱلۡكِتَٰبَ إِلَّا مِنۢ بَعۡدِ مَا جَآءَتۡهُمُ

ٱلۡبَيِّنَةُ ۝ وَمَآ أُمِرُوٓاْ إِلَّا لِيَعۡبُدُواْ ٱللَّهَ مُخۡلِصِينَ لَهُ ٱلدِّينَ

حُنَفَآءَ وَيُقِيمُواْ ٱلصَّلَوٰةَ وَيُؤۡتُواْ ٱلزَّكَوٰةَۚ وَذَٰلِكَ دِينُ ٱلۡقَيِّمَةِ ۝

إِنَّ ٱلَّذِينَ كَفَرُواْ مِنۡ أَهۡلِ ٱلۡكِتَٰبِ وَٱلۡمُشۡرِكِينَ فِي نَارِ جَهَنَّمَ

خَٰلِدِينَ فِيهَآۚ أُوْلَٰٓئِكَ هُمۡ شَرُّ ٱلۡبَرِيَّةِ ۝ إِنَّ ٱلَّذِينَ ءَامَنُواْ

وَعَمِلُواْ ٱلصَّٰلِحَٰتِ أُوْلَٰٓئِكَ هُمۡ خَيۡرُ ٱلۡبَرِيَّةِ ۝ جَزَآؤُهُمۡ

عِندَ رَبِّهِمۡ جَنَّٰتُ عَدۡنٖ تَجۡرِي مِن تَحۡتِهَا ٱلۡأَنۡهَٰرُ خَٰلِدِينَ

فِيهَآ أَبَدٗاۖ رَّضِيَ ٱللَّهُ عَنۡهُمۡ وَرَضُواْ عَنۡهُۚ ذَٰلِكَ لِمَنۡ خَشِيَ رَبَّهُۥ ۝

1. Indeed, We sent the Qur'an down during the Night of Decree.

2. And what can make you know what is the Night of Decree?

3. The Night of Decree is better than a thousand months.

4. The angels and the Spirit descend therein by permission of their Lord for every matter.

5. Peace it is until the emergence of dawn.

سورة القدر

Surāt Al-Qadr | The Night of Decree [97]

بِسْمِ ٱللَّهِ ٱلرَّحْمَٰنِ ٱلرَّحِيمِ

إِنَّا أَنزَلْنَٰهُ فِى لَيْلَةِ ٱلْقَدْرِ ۝١ وَمَآ أَدْرَىٰكَ مَا لَيْلَةُ ٱلْقَدْرِ ۝٢

لَيْلَةُ ٱلْقَدْرِ خَيْرٌ مِّنْ أَلْفِ شَهْرٍ ۝٣ تَنَزَّلُ ٱلْمَلَٰٓئِكَةُ وَٱلرُّوحُ فِيهَا

بِإِذْنِ رَبِّهِم مِّن كُلِّ أَمْرٍ ۝٤ سَلَٰمٌ هِىَ حَتَّىٰ مَطْلَعِ ٱلْفَجْرِ ۝٥

1. Read in the name of your Lord who created –

2. Created man from a clinging substance.

3. Read, and your Lord is the most Generous –

4. Who taught by the pen –

5. Taught man that which he knew not.

6. No! [But] indeed, man transgresses

7. Because he sees himself self-sufficient.

8. Indeed, to your Lord is the return.

9. Have you seen the one who forbids

10. A servant when he prays?

11. Have you seen if he is upon guidance

12. Or enjoins righteousness?

13. Have you seen if he denies and turns away –

14. Does he not know that Allah sees?

15. No! If he does not desist, We will surely drag him by the forelock –

16. A lying, sinning forelock.

17. Then let him call his associates;

18. We will call the angels of Hell.

19. No! Do not obey him. But prostrate and draw near [to Allah].

سورة العلق

Surāt Al-ʿAlaq | The Clot [96]

بِسْمِ اللَّهِ الرَّحْمَٰنِ الرَّحِيمِ

ٱقْرَأْ بِٱسْمِ رَبِّكَ ٱلَّذِي خَلَقَ ﴿١﴾ خَلَقَ ٱلْإِنسَٰنَ مِنْ عَلَقٍ ﴿٢﴾ ٱقْرَأْ وَرَبُّكَ ٱلْأَكْرَمُ ﴿٣﴾ ٱلَّذِي عَلَّمَ بِٱلْقَلَمِ ﴿٤﴾ عَلَّمَ ٱلْإِنسَٰنَ مَا لَمْ يَعْلَمْ ﴿٥﴾ كَلَّآ إِنَّ ٱلْإِنسَٰنَ لَيَطْغَىٰٓ ﴿٦﴾ أَن رَّءَاهُ ٱسْتَغْنَىٰٓ ﴿٧﴾ إِنَّ إِلَىٰ رَبِّكَ ٱلرُّجْعَىٰٓ ﴿٨﴾ أَرَءَيْتَ ٱلَّذِي يَنْهَىٰ ﴿٩﴾ عَبْدًا إِذَا صَلَّىٰٓ ﴿١٠﴾ أَرَءَيْتَ إِن كَانَ عَلَى ٱلْهُدَىٰٓ ﴿١١﴾ أَوْ أَمَرَ بِٱلتَّقْوَىٰٓ ﴿١٢﴾ أَرَءَيْتَ إِن كَذَّبَ وَتَوَلَّىٰٓ ﴿١٣﴾ أَلَمْ يَعْلَم بِأَنَّ ٱللَّهَ يَرَىٰ ﴿١٤﴾ كَلَّا لَئِن لَّمْ يَنتَهِ لَنَسْفَعًۢا بِٱلنَّاصِيَةِ ﴿١٥﴾ نَاصِيَةٍ كَٰذِبَةٍ خَاطِئَةٍ ﴿١٦﴾ فَلْيَدْعُ نَادِيَهُۥ ﴿١٧﴾ سَنَدْعُ ٱلزَّبَانِيَةَ ﴿١٨﴾ كَلَّا لَا تُطِعْهُ وَٱسْجُدْ وَٱقْتَرِب ۩ ﴿١٩﴾

When you come to this verse, it is Sunnah to perform sajdat al-tilāwah (the prostration of recitation).

1. By the fig and the olive

2. And [by] Mount Sinai

3. And [by] this secure city [Makkah],

4. We have certainly created man in the best of stature;

5. Then We return him to the lowest of the low,

6. Except for those who believe and do righteous deeds, for they will have a reward uninterrupted.

7. So what yet causes you to deny the Recompense?

8. Is not Allah the most just of judges?

سورة التين

Surāt At-Tīn | The Fig [95]

بِسْمِ اللَّهِ الرَّحْمَٰنِ الرَّحِيمِ

وَالتِّينِ وَالزَّيْتُونِ ۝ وَطُورِ سِينِينَ ۝ وَهَٰذَا الْبَلَدِ الْأَمِينِ ۝

لَقَدْ خَلَقْنَا الْإِنسَانَ فِي أَحْسَنِ تَقْوِيمٍ ۝ ثُمَّ رَدَدْنَاهُ أَسْفَلَ سَافِلِينَ

۝ إِلَّا الَّذِينَ آمَنُوا وَعَمِلُوا الصَّالِحَاتِ فَلَهُمْ أَجْرٌ غَيْرُ مَمْنُونٍ ۝

فَمَا يُكَذِّبُكَ بَعْدُ بِالدِّينِ ۝ أَلَيْسَ اللَّهُ بِأَحْكَمِ الْحَاكِمِينَ ۝

51

1. Did We not expand for you, [O Muhammad], your breast?

2. And We removed from you your burden

3. Which had weighed upon your back

4. And raised high for you your repute.

5. For indeed, with hardship [will be] ease.

6. Indeed, with hardship [will be] ease.

7. So when you have finished [your duties], then stand up [for worship].

8. And to your Lord direct [your] longing.

سورة الشرح

Surāt Ash-Sharḥ | The Relief / The Expansion [94]

بِسْمِ اللَّهِ الرَّحْمَٰنِ الرَّحِيمِ

أَلَمْ نَشْرَحْ لَكَ صَدْرَكَ ﴿١﴾ وَوَضَعْنَا عَنكَ وِزْرَكَ ﴿٢﴾

ٱلَّذِىٓ أَنقَضَ ظَهْرَكَ ﴿٣﴾ وَرَفَعْنَا لَكَ ذِكْرَكَ ﴿٤﴾ فَإِنَّ مَعَ ٱلْعُسْرِ يُسْرًا ﴿٥﴾

إِنَّ مَعَ ٱلْعُسْرِ يُسْرًا ﴿٦﴾ فَإِذَا فَرَغْتَ فَٱنصَبْ ﴿٧﴾ وَإِلَىٰ رَبِّكَ فَٱرْغَب ﴿٨﴾

1. By the morning brightness

2. And [by] the night when it covers with darkness,

3. Your Lord has not taken leave of you, [O Muhammad], nor has He detested [you].

4. And the Hereafter is better for you than the first [life].

5. And your Lord is going to give you, and you will be satisfied.

6. Did He not find you an orphan and give [you] refuge?

7. And He found you lost and guided [you],

8. And He found you poor and made [you] self-sufficient.

9. So as for the orphan, do not oppress [him].

10. And as for the petitioner, do not repel [him].

11. But as for the favour of your Lord, report [it].

سورة الضحى

Surāt Aḍ-Ḍuḥā | The Morning Brightness [94]

بِسْمِ اللَّهِ الرَّحْمَٰنِ الرَّحِيمِ

وَالضُّحَىٰ ﴿١﴾ وَاللَّيْلِ إِذَا سَجَىٰ ﴿٢﴾ مَا وَدَّعَكَ رَبُّكَ وَمَا قَلَىٰ ﴿٣﴾

وَلَلْآخِرَةُ خَيْرٌ لَّكَ مِنَ الْأُولَىٰ ﴿٤﴾ وَلَسَوْفَ يُعْطِيكَ رَبُّكَ

فَتَرْضَىٰ ﴿٥﴾ أَلَمْ يَجِدْكَ يَتِيمًا فَآوَىٰ ﴿٦﴾ وَوَجَدَكَ ضَالًّا فَهَدَىٰ

﴿٧﴾ وَوَجَدَكَ عَائِلًا فَأَغْنَىٰ ﴿٨﴾ فَأَمَّا الْيَتِيمَ فَلَا تَقْهَرْ ﴿٩﴾

وَأَمَّا السَّائِلَ فَلَا تَنْهَرْ ﴿١٠﴾ وَأَمَّا بِنِعْمَةِ رَبِّكَ فَحَدِّثْ ﴿١١﴾

1. By the night when it covers,

2. And [by] the day when it appears,

3. And [by] He who created the male and female,

4. Indeed, your efforts are diverse.

5. As for he who gives and fears Allah

6. And believes in the best [reward],

7. We will ease him toward ease.

8. But as for he who withholds and considers himself free of need

9. And denies the best [reward],

10. We will ease him toward difficulty.

11. And what will his wealth avail him when he falls?

12. Indeed, [incumbent] upon Us is guidance.

13. And indeed, to Us belongs the Hereafter and the first [life].

14. So I have warned you of a Fire which is blazing.

15. None will [enter to] burn therein except the most wretched one

16. Who had denied and turned away.

17. But the righteous one will avoid it –

18. [He] who gives [from] his wealth to purify himself

19. And not [giving] for anyone who has [done him] a favour to be rewarded

20. But only seeking the Face of his Lord, Most High.

21. And he is going to be satisfied.

سورة الليل

Surāt Al-Layl | The Night [92]

بسم الله الرحمن الرحيم

وَالَّيْلِ إِذَا يَغْشَىٰ ۝١ وَالنَّهَارِ إِذَا تَجَلَّىٰ ۝٢ وَمَا خَلَقَ الذَّكَرَ وَالْأُنثَىٰ ۝٣

إِنَّ سَعْيَكُمْ لَشَتَّىٰ ۝٤ فَأَمَّا مَنْ أَعْطَىٰ وَاتَّقَىٰ ۝٥ وَصَدَّقَ بِالْحُسْنَىٰ ۝٦

فَسَنُيَسِّرُهُ لِلْيُسْرَىٰ ۝٧ وَأَمَّا مَنۢ بَخِلَ وَاسْتَغْنَىٰ ۝٨ وَكَذَّبَ بِالْحُسْنَىٰ ۝٩

فَسَنُيَسِّرُهُ لِلْعُسْرَىٰ ۝١٠ وَمَا يُغْنِي عَنْهُ مَالُهُۥٓ إِذَا تَرَدَّىٰ ۝١١ إِنَّ عَلَيْنَا

لَلْهُدَىٰ ۝١٢ وَإِنَّ لَنَا لَلْءَاخِرَةَ وَالْأُولَىٰ ۝١٣ فَأَنذَرْتُكُمْ نَارًا تَلَظَّىٰ ۝١٤

لَا يَصْلَىٰهَآ إِلَّا الْأَشْقَى ۝١٥ الَّذِي كَذَّبَ وَتَوَلَّىٰ ۝١٦ وَسَيُجَنَّبُهَا

الْأَتْقَى ۝١٧ الَّذِي يُؤْتِي مَالَهُۥ يَتَزَكَّىٰ ۝١٨ وَمَا لِأَحَدٍ عِندَهُۥ مِن نِّعْمَةٍ

تُجْزَىٰٓ ۝١٩ إِلَّا ابْتِغَآءَ وَجْهِ رَبِّهِ الْأَعْلَىٰ ۝٢٠ وَلَسَوْفَ يَرْضَىٰ ۝٢١

1. By the sun and its brightness,

2. And [by] the moon when it follows it,

3. And [by] the day when it displays it,

4. And [by] the night when it covers it,

5. And [by] the sky and He who constructed it,

6. And [by] the earth and He who spread it,

7. And [by] the soul and He who proportioned it

8. And inspired it [with discernment of] its wickedness and its righteousness,

9. He has succeeded who purifies it,

10. And he has failed who instills it [with corruption].

سورة الشمس

Surāt Ash-Shams | The Sun [91]

بسم الله الرحمن الرحيم

وَالشَّمْسِ وَضُحَىٰهَا ﴿١﴾ وَالْقَمَرِ إِذَا تَلَىٰهَا ﴿٢﴾ وَالنَّهَارِ إِذَا جَلَّىٰهَا ﴿٣﴾ وَاللَّيْلِ إِذَا يَغْشَىٰهَا ﴿٤﴾ وَالسَّمَاءِ وَمَا بَنَىٰهَا ﴿٥﴾ وَالْأَرْضِ وَمَا طَحَىٰهَا ﴿٦﴾ وَنَفْسٍ وَمَا سَوَّىٰهَا ﴿٧﴾ فَأَلْهَمَهَا فُجُورَهَا وَتَقْوَىٰهَا ﴿٨﴾ قَدْ أَفْلَحَ مَن زَكَّىٰهَا ﴿٩﴾ وَقَدْ خَابَ مَن دَسَّىٰهَا ﴿١٠﴾ كَذَّبَتْ ثَمُودُ بِطَغْوَىٰهَا ﴿١١﴾ إِذِ انبَعَثَ أَشْقَىٰهَا ﴿١٢﴾ فَقَالَ لَهُمْ رَسُولُ اللَّهِ نَاقَةَ اللَّهِ وَسُقْيَىٰهَا ﴿١٣﴾ فَكَذَّبُوهُ فَعَقَرُوهَا فَدَمْدَمَ عَلَيْهِمْ رَبُّهُم بِذَنبِهِمْ فَسَوَّىٰهَا ﴿١٤﴾ وَلَا يَخَافُ عُقْبَىٰهَا ﴿١٥﴾

1. I swear by this city –

2. And you, [O Muhammad], are free of restriction in this city –

3. And [by] the father and that which was born [of him],

4. We have certainly created man into hardship.

5. Does he think that never will anyone overcome him?

6. He says, "I have spent wealth in abundance."

7. Does he think that no one has seen him?

8. Have We not made for him two eyes?

9. And a tongue and two lips?

10. And have shown him the two ways?

11. But he has not broken through the difficult pass.

12. And what can make you know what is [breaking through] the difficult pass?

13. It is the freeing of a slave

14. Or feeding on a day of severe hunger

15. An orphan of near relationship

16. Or a needy person in misery

17. And then being among those who believed and advised one another to patience and advised one another to compassion

18. Those are the companions of the right.

19. But they who disbelieved in Our signs – those are the companions of the left.

20. Over them will be fire closed in.

سورة البلد

Surāt Al-Balad | The City [90]

بِسْمِ اللَّهِ الرَّحْمَٰنِ الرَّحِيمِ

لَا أُقْسِمُ بِهَٰذَا الْبَلَدِ ﴿١﴾ وَأَنتَ حِلٌّ بِهَٰذَا الْبَلَدِ ﴿٢﴾ وَوَالِدٍ وَمَا وَلَدَ ﴿٣﴾ لَقَدْ خَلَقْنَا الْإِنسَانَ فِي كَبَدٍ ﴿٤﴾ أَيَحْسَبُ أَن لَّن يَقْدِرَ عَلَيْهِ أَحَدٌ ﴿٥﴾ يَقُولُ أَهْلَكْتُ مَالًا لُّبَدًا ﴿٦﴾ أَيَحْسَبُ أَن لَّمْ يَرَهُ أَحَدٌ ﴿٧﴾ أَلَمْ نَجْعَل لَّهُ عَيْنَيْنِ ﴿٨﴾ وَلِسَانًا وَشَفَتَيْنِ ﴿٩﴾ وَهَدَيْنَاهُ النَّجْدَيْنِ ﴿١٠﴾ فَلَا اقْتَحَمَ الْعَقَبَةَ ﴿١١﴾ وَمَا أَدْرَاكَ مَا الْعَقَبَةُ ﴿١٢﴾ فَكُّ رَقَبَةٍ ﴿١٣﴾ أَوْ إِطْعَامٌ فِي يَوْمٍ ذِي مَسْغَبَةٍ ﴿١٤﴾ يَتِيمًا ذَا مَقْرَبَةٍ ﴿١٥﴾ أَوْ مِسْكِينًا ذَا مَتْرَبَةٍ ﴿١٦﴾ ثُمَّ كَانَ مِنَ الَّذِينَ آمَنُوا وَتَوَاصَوْا بِالصَّبْرِ وَتَوَاصَوْا بِالْمَرْحَمَةِ ﴿١٧﴾ أُولَٰئِكَ أَصْحَابُ الْمَيْمَنَةِ ﴿١٨﴾ وَالَّذِينَ كَفَرُوا بِآيَاتِنَا هُمْ أَصْحَابُ الْمَشْأَمَةِ ﴿١٩﴾ عَلَيْهِمْ نَارٌ مُّؤْصَدَةٌ ﴿٢٠﴾

1. By the dawn

2. And [by] ten nights

3. And [by] the even [number] and the odd

4. And [by] the night when it passes,

5. Is there [not] in [all] that an oath [sufficient] for one of perception?

6. Have you not considered how your Lord dealt with 'Aad –

7. [With] Iram – who had lofty pillars,

8. The likes of whom had never been created in the land?

9. And [with] Thamud, who carved out the rocks in the valley?

10. And [with] Pharaoh, owner of the stakes?

11. [All of] whom oppressed within the lands

12. And increased therein the corruption.

13. So your Lord poured upon them a scourge of punishment.

14. Indeed, your Lord is in observation.

15. And as for man, when his Lord tries him and [thus] is generous to him and favours him, he says, "My Lord has honoured me."

16. But when He tries him and restricts his provision, he says, "My Lord has humiliated me."

17. No! But you do not honour the orphan

18. And you do not encourage one another to feed the poor.

سورة الفجر

Surāt Al-Fajr | The Dawn [89] | Part 1

بِسْمِ اللَّهِ الرَّحْمَٰنِ الرَّحِيمِ

وَالْفَجْرِ ﴿١﴾ وَلَيَالٍ عَشْرٍ ﴿٢﴾ وَالشَّفْعِ وَالْوَتْرِ ﴿٣﴾ وَاللَّيْلِ إِذَا يَسْرِ ﴿٤﴾

هَلْ فِي ذَٰلِكَ قَسَمٌ لِّذِي حِجْرٍ ﴿٥﴾ أَلَمْ تَرَ كَيْفَ فَعَلَ رَبُّكَ بِعَادٍ ﴿٦﴾

إِرَمَ ذَاتِ الْعِمَادِ ﴿٧﴾ الَّتِي لَمْ يُخْلَقْ مِثْلُهَا فِي الْبِلَادِ ﴿٨﴾ وَثَمُودَ الَّذِينَ

جَابُوا الصَّخْرَ بِالْوَادِ ﴿٩﴾ وَفِرْعَوْنَ ذِي الْأَوْتَادِ ﴿١٠﴾ الَّذِينَ طَغَوْا فِي

الْبِلَادِ ﴿١١﴾ فَأَكْثَرُوا فِيهَا الْفَسَادَ ﴿١٢﴾ فَصَبَّ عَلَيْهِمْ رَبُّكَ سَوْطَ

عَذَابٍ ﴿١٣﴾ إِنَّ رَبَّكَ لَبِالْمِرْصَادِ ﴿١٤﴾ فَأَمَّا الْإِنسَانُ إِذَا مَا ابْتَلَاهُ

رَبُّهُ فَأَكْرَمَهُ وَنَعَّمَهُ فَيَقُولُ رَبِّي أَكْرَمَنِ ﴿١٥﴾ وَأَمَّا إِذَا مَا ابْتَلَاهُ

فَقَدَرَ عَلَيْهِ رِزْقَهُ فَيَقُولُ رَبِّي أَهَانَنِ ﴿١٦﴾ كَلَّا ۖ بَل لَّا تُكْرِمُونَ

الْيَتِيمَ ﴿١٧﴾ وَلَا تَحَاضُّونَ عَلَىٰ طَعَامِ الْمِسْكِينِ ﴿١٨﴾ وَتَأْكُلُونَ

19. And you consume inheritance greedily

20. And you love wealth with immense love.

21. No! When the earth has been levelled – pounded and crushed –

22. And your Lord has come and the angels, rank upon rank,

23. And brought [within view], that Day, is Hell – that Day, man will remember, but how will that remembrance [then] avail him?

24. He will say, "Oh, I wish I had sent ahead [some good] for my life."

25. So on that Day, none will punish [as severely] as His punishment,

26. And none will bind [as severely] as His binding [of the evildoers].

27. O tranquil soul,

28. Return to your Lord, well-pleased and pleasing [to Him],

29. And enter among My [righteous] servants,

30. And enter My Paradise

ٱلتُّرَاثَ أَكْلًا لَّمًّا ﴿١٩﴾ وَتُحِبُّونَ ٱلْمَالَ حُبًّا جَمًّا ﴿٢٠﴾ كَلَّا إِذَا دُكَّتِ ٱلْأَرْضُ دَكًّا دَكًّا ﴿٢١﴾ وَجَاءَ رَبُّكَ وَٱلْمَلَكُ صَفًّا صَفًّا ﴿٢٢﴾ وَجِائَ يَوْمَئِذٍ بِجَهَنَّمَ يَوْمَئِذٍ يَتَذَكَّرُ ٱلْإِنسَانُ وَأَنَّىٰ لَهُ ٱلذِّكْرَىٰ ﴿٢٣﴾ يَقُولُ يَٰلَيْتَنِى قَدَّمْتُ لِحَيَاتِى ﴿٢٤﴾ فَيَوْمَئِذٍ لَّا يُعَذِّبُ عَذَابَهُ أَحَدٌ ﴿٢٥﴾ وَلَا يُوثِقُ وَثَاقَهُ أَحَدٌ ﴿٢٦﴾ يَٰٓأَيَّتُهَا ٱلنَّفْسُ ٱلْمُطْمَئِنَّةُ ﴿٢٧﴾ ٱرْجِعِى إِلَىٰ رَبِّكِ رَاضِيَةً مَّرْضِيَّةً ﴿٢٨﴾ فَٱدْخُلِى فِى عِبَادِى ﴿٢٩﴾ وَٱدْخُلِى جَنَّتِى ﴿٣٠﴾

1. Has there reached you the report of the Overwhelming [event]?

2. Some faces, that Day, will be humbled,

3. Working [hard] and exhausted.

4. They will [enter to] burn in an intensely hot Fire.

5. They will be given drink from a boiling spring.

6. For them there will be no food except from a poisonous, thorny plant

7. Which neither nourishes nor avails against hunger.

8. [Other] faces, that Day, will show pleasure.

9. With their effort [they are] satisfied

10. In an elevated garden,

11. Wherein they will hear no unsuitable speech.

12. Within it is a flowing spring.

13. Within it are couches raised

14. And cups set at hand

15. And cushions lined

16. And carpets spread.

17. Do they not look at the camels – how they are created?

18. And at the sky – how it is raised?

19. And at the mountains – how they are erected?

20. And at the earth – how it is spread out?

21. So remind, [O Muhammad]; you are only a reminder.

22. You are not over them a controller.

23. However, he who turns away and disbelieves –

24. Allah will punish him with the greatest punishment.

25. Indeed, to Us is their return.

26. Then indeed, upon Us is their account.

سورة الغاشية

Surāt Al-Ghāshiyah | The Overwhelming [88]

بِسْمِ اللَّهِ الرَّحْمَٰنِ الرَّحِيمِ

هَلْ أَتَاكَ حَدِيثُ الْغَاشِيَةِ ﴿١﴾ وُجُوهٌ يَوْمَئِذٍ خَاشِعَةٌ ﴿٢﴾ عَامِلَةٌ نَّاصِبَةٌ ﴿٣﴾ تَصْلَىٰ نَارًا حَامِيَةً ﴿٤﴾ تُسْقَىٰ مِنْ عَيْنٍ آنِيَةٍ ﴿٥﴾ لَّيْسَ لَهُمْ طَعَامٌ إِلَّا مِن ضَرِيعٍ ﴿٦﴾ لَّا يُسْمِنُ وَلَا يُغْنِي مِن جُوعٍ ﴿٧﴾ وُجُوهٌ يَوْمَئِذٍ نَّاعِمَةٌ ﴿٨﴾ لِّسَعْيِهَا رَاضِيَةٌ ﴿٩﴾ فِي جَنَّةٍ عَالِيَةٍ ﴿١٠﴾ لَّا تَسْمَعُ فِيهَا لَاغِيَةً ﴿١١﴾ فِيهَا عَيْنٌ جَارِيَةٌ ﴿١٢﴾ فِيهَا سُرُرٌ مَّرْفُوعَةٌ ﴿١٣﴾ وَأَكْوَابٌ مَّوْضُوعَةٌ ﴿١٤﴾ وَنَمَارِقُ مَصْفُوفَةٌ ﴿١٥﴾ وَزَرَابِيُّ مَبْثُوثَةٌ ﴿١٦﴾ أَفَلَا يَنظُرُونَ إِلَى الْإِبِلِ كَيْفَ خُلِقَتْ ﴿١٧﴾ وَإِلَى السَّمَاءِ كَيْفَ رُفِعَتْ ﴿١٨﴾ وَإِلَى الْجِبَالِ كَيْفَ نُصِبَتْ ﴿١٩﴾ وَإِلَى الْأَرْضِ كَيْفَ سُطِحَتْ ﴿٢٠﴾ فَذَكِّرْ إِنَّمَا أَنتَ مُذَكِّرٌ ﴿٢١﴾ لَّسْتَ عَلَيْهِم بِمُصَيْطِرٍ ﴿٢٢﴾ إِلَّا مَن تَوَلَّىٰ وَكَفَرَ ﴿٢٣﴾ فَيُعَذِّبُهُ اللَّهُ الْعَذَابَ الْأَكْبَرَ ﴿٢٤﴾ إِنَّ إِلَيْنَا إِيَابَهُمْ ﴿٢٥﴾ ثُمَّ إِنَّ عَلَيْنَا حِسَابَهُم ﴿٢٦﴾

1. Exalt the name of your Lord, the Most High,

2. Who created and proportioned

3. And who destined and [then] guided

4. And who brings out the pasture

5. And then makes it black stubble.

6. We will make you recite, [O Muhammad], and you will not forget,

7. Except what Allah should will. Indeed, He knows what is declared and what is hidden.

8. And We will ease you toward ease.

9. So remind, if the reminder should benefit;

10. He who fears [Allah] will be reminded.

11. But the wretched one will avoid it –

12. [He] who will [enter and] burn in the greatest Fire,

13. Neither dying therein nor living.

14. He has certainly succeeded who purifies himself

15. And mentions the name of his Lord and prays.

16. But you prefer the worldly life,

17. While the Hereafter is better and more enduring.

18. Indeed, this is in the former scriptures,

19. The scriptures of Abraham and Moses.

سورة الأعلى

Surāt Al-A'lā | The Most High [87]

بِسْمِ اللَّهِ الرَّحْمَٰنِ الرَّحِيمِ

سَبِّحِ اسْمَ رَبِّكَ الْأَعْلَى ﴿١﴾ الَّذِي خَلَقَ فَسَوَّىٰ ﴿٢﴾ وَالَّذِي قَدَّرَ فَهَدَىٰ ﴿٣﴾ وَالَّذِي أَخْرَجَ الْمَرْعَىٰ ﴿٤﴾ فَجَعَلَهُ غُثَاءً أَحْوَىٰ ﴿٥﴾ سَنُقْرِئُكَ فَلَا تَنسَىٰ ﴿٦﴾ إِلَّا مَا شَاءَ اللَّهُ ۚ إِنَّهُ يَعْلَمُ الْجَهْرَ وَمَا يَخْفَىٰ ﴿٧﴾ وَنُيَسِّرُكَ لِلْيُسْرَىٰ ﴿٨﴾ فَذَكِّرْ إِن نَّفَعَتِ الذِّكْرَىٰ ﴿٩﴾ سَيَذَّكَّرُ مَن يَخْشَىٰ ﴿١٠﴾ وَيَتَجَنَّبُهَا الْأَشْقَى ﴿١١﴾ الَّذِي يَصْلَى النَّارَ الْكُبْرَىٰ ﴿١٢﴾ ثُمَّ لَا يَمُوتُ فِيهَا وَلَا يَحْيَىٰ ﴿١٣﴾ قَدْ أَفْلَحَ مَن تَزَكَّىٰ ﴿١٤﴾ وَذَكَرَ اسْمَ رَبِّهِ فَصَلَّىٰ ﴿١٥﴾ بَلْ تُؤْثِرُونَ الْحَيَاةَ الدُّنْيَا ﴿١٦﴾ وَالْآخِرَةُ خَيْرٌ وَأَبْقَىٰ ﴿١٧﴾ إِنَّ هَٰذَا لَفِي الصُّحُفِ الْأُولَىٰ ﴿١٨﴾ صُحُفِ إِبْرَاهِيمَ وَمُوسَىٰ ﴿١٩﴾

1. By the sky and the night comer –

2. And what can make you know what is the night comer?

3. It is the piercing star –

4. There is no soul but that it has over it a protector.

5. So let man observe from what he was created.

6. He was created from a fluid, ejected,

7. Emerging from between the backbone and the ribs.

8. Indeed, Allah, to return him [to life], is Able.

9. The Day when secrets will be put on trial,

10. Then man will have no power or any helper.

11. By the sky which returns [rain]

12. And [by] the earth which cracks open,

13. Indeed, the Qur'an is a decisive statement,

14. And it is not amusement.

15. Indeed, they are planning a plan,

16. But I am planning a plan.

17. So allow time for the disbelievers. Leave them awhile.

سورة الطارق

Surāt Aṭ-Ṭāriq | The Morning Star [86]

بِسْمِ اللَّهِ الرَّحْمَٰنِ الرَّحِيمِ

وَالسَّمَاءِ وَالطَّارِقِ ﴿١﴾ وَمَا أَدْرَاكَ مَا الطَّارِقُ ﴿٢﴾ النَّجْمُ الثَّاقِبُ ﴿٣﴾ إِن كُلُّ نَفْسٍ لَّمَّا عَلَيْهَا حَافِظٌ ﴿٤﴾ فَلْيَنظُرِ الْإِنسَانُ مِمَّ خُلِقَ ﴿٥﴾ خُلِقَ مِن مَّاءٍ دَافِقٍ ﴿٦﴾ يَخْرُجُ مِن بَيْنِ الصُّلْبِ وَالتَّرَائِبِ ﴿٧﴾ إِنَّهُ عَلَىٰ رَجْعِهِ لَقَادِرٌ ﴿٨﴾ يَوْمَ تُبْلَى السَّرَائِرُ ﴿٩﴾ فَمَا لَهُ مِن قُوَّةٍ وَلَا نَاصِرٍ ﴿١٠﴾ وَالسَّمَاءِ ذَاتِ الرَّجْعِ ﴿١١﴾ وَالْأَرْضِ ذَاتِ الصَّدْعِ ﴿١٢﴾ إِنَّهُ لَقَوْلٌ فَصْلٌ ﴿١٣﴾ وَمَا هُوَ بِالْهَزْلِ ﴿١٤﴾ إِنَّهُمْ يَكِيدُونَ كَيْدًا ﴿١٥﴾ وَأَكِيدُ كَيْدًا ﴿١٦﴾ فَمَهِّلِ الْكَافِرِينَ أَمْهِلْهُمْ رُوَيْدًا ﴿١٧﴾

1. By the sky containing great stars

2. And [by] the promised Day

3. And [by] the witness and what is witnessed,

4. Cursed were the companions of the trench

5. [Containing] the fire full of fuel,

6. When they were sitting near it

7. And they, to what they were doing against the believers, were witnesses.

8. And they resented them not except because they believed in Allah, the Exalted in Might, the Praiseworthy,

9. To whom belongs the dominion of the heavens and the earth. And Allah, over all things, is Witness.

10. Indeed, those who have tortured the believing men and believing women and then have not repented will have the punishment of Hell, and they will have the punishment of the Burning Fire.

11. Indeed, those who have believed and done righteous deeds will have gardens beneath which rivers flow. That is the great attainment.

12. Indeed, the assault of your Lord is severe.

13. Indeed, it is He who originates [creation] and repeats.

14. And He is the Forgiving, the Affectionate,

15. Honourable Owner of the Throne,

16. Effecter of what He intends.

17. Has there reached you the story of the soldiers –

18. [Those of] Pharaoh and Thamūd?

19. But they who disbelieve are in [persistent] denial,

20. While Allah encompasses them from behind.

21. But this is an honoured Qur'an

22. [Inscribed] in a Preserved Slate.

سورة البروج

Surāt Al-Burūj | The Mansions of the Stars [85]

بِسْمِ اللهِ الرَّحْمَنِ الرَّحِيمِ

وَالسَّمَاءِ ذَاتِ الْبُرُوجِ ۝ وَالْيَوْمِ الْمَوْعُودِ ۝ وَشَاهِدٍ وَمَشْهُودٍ ۝ قُتِلَ أَصْحَابُ الْأُخْدُودِ ۝ النَّارِ ذَاتِ الْوَقُودِ ۝ إِذْ هُمْ عَلَيْهَا قُعُودٌ ۝ وَهُمْ عَلَى مَا يَفْعَلُونَ بِالْمُؤْمِنِينَ شُهُودٌ ۝ وَمَا نَقَمُوا مِنْهُمْ إِلَّا أَن يُؤْمِنُوا بِاللهِ الْعَزِيزِ الْحَمِيدِ ۝ الَّذِي لَهُ مُلْكُ السَّمَوَاتِ وَالْأَرْضِ وَاللهُ عَلَى كُلِّ شَيْءٍ شَهِيدٌ ۝ إِنَّ الَّذِينَ فَتَنُوا الْمُؤْمِنِينَ وَالْمُؤْمِنَاتِ ثُمَّ لَمْ يَتُوبُوا فَلَهُمْ عَذَابُ جَهَنَّمَ وَلَهُمْ عَذَابُ الْحَرِيقِ ۝ إِنَّ الَّذِينَ آمَنُوا وَعَمِلُوا الصَّالِحَاتِ لَهُمْ جَنَّاتٌ تَجْرِي مِن تَحْتِهَا الْأَنْهَارُ ذَلِكَ الْفَوْزُ الْكَبِيرُ ۝ إِنَّ بَطْشَ رَبِّكَ لَشَدِيدٌ ۝ إِنَّهُ هُوَ يُبْدِئُ وَيُعِيدُ ۝ وَهُوَ الْغَفُورُ الْوَدُودُ ۝ ذُو الْعَرْشِ الْمَجِيدُ ۝ فَعَّالٌ لِّمَا يُرِيدُ ۝ هَلْ أَتَاكَ حَدِيثُ الْجُنُودِ ۝ فِرْعَوْنَ وَثَمُودَ ۝ بَلِ الَّذِينَ كَفَرُوا فِي تَكْذِيبٍ ۝ وَاللهُ مِن وَرَائِهِم مُّحِيطٌ ۝ بَلْ هُوَ قُرْآنٌ مَّجِيدٌ ۝ فِي لَوْحٍ مَّحْفُوظٍ ۝

1.   When the sky has split open

2.   And has responded to its Lord and was obligated [to do so]

3.   And when the earth has been extended

4.   And has cast out that within it and relinquished [it],

5.   And has responded to its Lord and was obligated [to do so]

6.   O mankind, indeed you are labouring toward your Lord with [great] exertion and will meet it.

7.   So whoever is given his record in his right hand

8.   He will be judged with an easy account

9.   And return to his people in happiness.

10. But whoever is given his record behind his back

11. He will cry out for destruction

12. And [enter to] burn in a Blaze.

13. Indeed, he had [once] been among his people in happiness;

14. Indeed, he had thought he would never return [to Allah].

15. But yes! Indeed, his Lord was ever, of him, Seeing.

16. So I swear by the twilight glow

17. And by the night and what it envelops

18. And by the moon when it becomes full

19. You will surely journey from stage to stage.

20. Then what is [wrong] with them that they do not believe,

21. And when the Qur'an is recited to them, they do not prostrate?

22. But those who have disbelieved deny,

23. And Allah is most knowing of what they keep within themselves.

24. So give them tidings of a painful punishment,

25. Except for those who believe and do righteous deeds. For them is a reward uninterrupted.

سورة الإنشقاق

Surāt Al-Inshiqqāq | The Splitting Open [84]

بِسْمِ اللَّهِ الرَّحْمَٰنِ الرَّحِيمِ

إِذَا السَّمَاءُ انشَقَّتْ ﴿١﴾ وَأَذِنَتْ لِرَبِّهَا وَحُقَّتْ ﴿٢﴾ وَإِذَا الْأَرْضُ مُدَّتْ ﴿٣﴾ وَأَلْقَتْ مَا فِيهَا وَتَخَلَّتْ ﴿٤﴾ وَأَذِنَتْ لِرَبِّهَا وَحُقَّتْ ﴿٥﴾ يَا أَيُّهَا الْإِنسَانُ إِنَّكَ كَادِحٌ إِلَىٰ رَبِّكَ كَدْحًا فَمُلَاقِيهِ ﴿٦﴾ فَأَمَّا مَنْ أُوتِيَ كِتَابَهُ بِيَمِينِهِ ﴿٧﴾ فَسَوْفَ يُحَاسَبُ حِسَابًا يَسِيرًا ﴿٨﴾ وَيَنقَلِبُ إِلَىٰ أَهْلِهِ مَسْرُورًا ﴿٩﴾ وَأَمَّا مَنْ أُوتِيَ كِتَابَهُ وَرَاءَ ظَهْرِهِ ﴿١٠﴾ فَسَوْفَ يَدْعُو ثُبُورًا ﴿١١﴾ وَيَصْلَىٰ سَعِيرًا ﴿١٢﴾ إِنَّهُ كَانَ فِي أَهْلِهِ مَسْرُورًا ﴿١٣﴾ إِنَّهُ ظَنَّ أَن لَّن يَحُورَ ﴿١٤﴾ بَلَىٰ إِنَّ رَبَّهُ كَانَ بِهِ بَصِيرًا ﴿١٥﴾ فَلَا أُقْسِمُ بِالشَّفَقِ ﴿١٦﴾ وَاللَّيْلِ وَمَا وَسَقَ ﴿١٧﴾ وَالْقَمَرِ إِذَا اتَّسَقَ ﴿١٨﴾ لَتَرْكَبُنَّ طَبَقًا عَن طَبَقٍ ﴿١٩﴾ فَمَا لَهُمْ لَا يُؤْمِنُونَ ﴿٢٠﴾ وَإِذَا قُرِئَ عَلَيْهِمُ الْقُرْآنُ لَا يَسْجُدُونَ ۩ ﴿٢١﴾ بَلِ الَّذِينَ كَفَرُوا يُكَذِّبُونَ ﴿٢٢﴾ وَاللَّهُ أَعْلَمُ بِمَا يُوعُونَ ﴿٢٣﴾ فَبَشِّرْهُم بِعَذَابٍ أَلِيمٍ ﴿٢٤﴾ إِلَّا الَّذِينَ آمَنُوا وَعَمِلُوا الصَّالِحَاتِ لَهُمْ أَجْرٌ غَيْرُ مَمْنُونٍ ﴿٢٥﴾

1. Woe to those that deal in fraud –

2. Those who, when they take a measure from people, take in full.

3. But if they give by measure or by weight to them, they cause loss.

4. Do they not think that they will be resurrected

5. For a tremendous Day –

6. The Day when mankind will stand before the Lord of the worlds?

7. No! Indeed, the record of the wicked is in Sijjeen.

8. And what can make you know what is Sijjeen?

9. It is [their destination recorded in] a register inscribed.

10. Woe, that Day, to the deniers,

11. Who deny the Day of Recompense.

12. And none deny it except every sinful transgressor.

13. When Our verses are recited to him, he says, "[Legends of] the former peoples."

14. No! Rather, the stain has covered their hearts of that which they were earning.

15. No! Indeed, from their Lord, that Day, they will be partitioned.

16. Then indeed, they will [enter and] burn in Hellfire.

17. Then it will be said [to them], "This is what you used to deny."

18. No! Indeed, the record of the righteous is in ʿilliyyīn.

19. And what can make you know what is ʿilliyyīn?

20. It is [their destination recorded in] a register inscribed

21. Which is witnessed by those brought near [to Allah].

22. Indeed, the righteous will be in pleasure

23. On adorned couches, observing.

سورة المطففين

Surat Al-Muṭaffifīn | Those Who Give Less / The Defrauding [83]

بِسْمِ ٱللَّهِ ٱلرَّحْمَٰنِ ٱلرَّحِيمِ

وَيْلٌ لِّلْمُطَفِّفِينَ ۝ ٱلَّذِينَ إِذَا ٱكْتَالُوا۟ عَلَى ٱلنَّاسِ يَسْتَوْفُونَ ۝ وَإِذَا كَالُوهُمْ أَو وَّزَنُوهُمْ يُخْسِرُونَ ۝ أَلَا يَظُنُّ أُو۟لَٰٓئِكَ أَنَّهُم مَّبْعُوثُونَ ۝ لِيَوْمٍ عَظِيمٍ ۝ يَوْمَ يَقُومُ ٱلنَّاسُ لِرَبِّ ٱلْعَٰلَمِينَ ۝ كَلَّآ إِنَّ كِتَٰبَ ٱلْفُجَّارِ لَفِى سِجِّينٍ ۝ وَمَآ أَدْرَىٰكَ مَا سِجِّينٌ ۝ كِتَٰبٌ مَّرْقُومٌ ۝ وَيْلٌ يَوْمَئِذٍ لِّلْمُكَذِّبِينَ ۝ ٱلَّذِينَ يُكَذِّبُونَ بِيَوْمِ ٱلدِّينِ ۝ وَمَا يُكَذِّبُ بِهِۦٓ إِلَّا كُلُّ مُعْتَدٍ أَثِيمٍ ۝ إِذَا تُتْلَىٰ عَلَيْهِ ءَايَٰتُنَا قَالَ أَسَٰطِيرُ ٱلْأَوَّلِينَ ۝ كَلَّا بَلْ رَانَ عَلَىٰ قُلُوبِهِم مَّا كَانُوا۟ يَكْسِبُونَ ۝ كَلَّآ إِنَّهُمْ عَن رَّبِّهِمْ يَوْمَئِذٍ لَّمَحْجُوبُونَ ۝ ثُمَّ إِنَّهُمْ لَصَالُوا۟ ٱلْجَحِيمِ ۝ ثُمَّ يُقَالُ هَٰذَا ٱلَّذِى كُنتُم بِهِۦ تُكَذِّبُونَ ۝ كَلَّآ إِنَّ كِتَٰبَ ٱلْأَبْرَارِ لَفِى عِلِّيِّينَ ۝ وَمَآ أَدْرَىٰكَ مَا عِلِّيُّونَ ۝ كِتَٰبٌ مَّرْقُومٌ ۝ يَشْهَدُهُ ٱلْمُقَرَّبُونَ ۝ إِنَّ ٱلْأَبْرَارَ لَفِى نَعِيمٍ ۝ عَلَى ٱلْأَرَآئِكِ يَنظُرُونَ ۝ تَعْرِفُ فِى

24. You will recognize in their faces the radiance of pleasure.

25. They will be given to drink [pure] wine [which was] sealed.

26. The last of it is musk. So for this let the competitors compete.

27. And its mixture is of Tasnīm –

28. A spring from which those near [to Allah] drink.

29. Indeed, those who committed crimes used to laugh at those who believed.

30. And when they passed by them, they would exchange derisive glances.

31. And when they returned to their people, they would return jesting.

32. And when they saw them, they would say, "Indeed, those are truly lost."

33. But they had not been sent as guardians over them.

34. So Today those who believed are laughing at the disbelievers

35. On adorned couches, observing.

36. Have the disbelievers [not] been rewarded [this Day] for what they used to do?

وُجُوهِهِمْ نَضْرَةَ ٱلنَّعِيمِ ۝ يُسْقَوْنَ مِن رَّحِيقٍ مَّخْتُومٍ ۝ خِتَٰمُهُۥ

مِسْكٌ ۚ وَفِى ذَٰلِكَ فَلْيَتَنَافَسِ ٱلْمُتَنَٰفِسُونَ ۝ وَمِزَاجُهُۥ مِن

تَسْنِيمٍ ۝ عَيْنًا يَشْرَبُ بِهَا ٱلْمُقَرَّبُونَ ۝ إِنَّ ٱلَّذِينَ أَجْرَمُوا۟ كَانُوا۟

مِنَ ٱلَّذِينَ ءَامَنُوا۟ يَضْحَكُونَ ۝ وَإِذَا مَرُّوا۟ بِهِمْ يَتَغَامَزُونَ ۝

وَإِذَا ٱنقَلَبُوٓا۟ إِلَىٰٓ أَهْلِهِمُ ٱنقَلَبُوا۟ فَكِهِينَ ۝ وَإِذَا رَأَوْهُمْ قَالُوٓا۟

إِنَّ هَٰٓؤُلَآءِ لَضَآلُّونَ ۝ وَمَآ أُرْسِلُوا۟ عَلَيْهِمْ حَٰفِظِينَ ۝

فَٱلْيَوْمَ ٱلَّذِينَ ءَامَنُوا۟ مِنَ ٱلْكُفَّارِ يَضْحَكُونَ ۝ عَلَى

ٱلْأَرَآئِكِ يَنظُرُونَ ۝ هَلْ ثُوِّبَ ٱلْكُفَّارُ مَا كَانُوا۟ يَفْعَلُونَ ۝

1. When the sky breaks apart

2. And when the stars fall, scattering,

3. And when the seas are erupted

4. And when the [contents of] graves are scattered,

5. A soul will [then] know what it has put forth and kept back.

6. O mankind, what has deceived you concerning your Lord, the Generous,

7. Who created you, proportioned you, and balanced you?

8. In whatever form He willed has He assembled you.

9. No! But you deny the Recompense.

10. And indeed, [appointed] over you are keepers,

11. Noble and recording;

12. They know whatever you do.

13. Indeed, the righteous will be in pleasure,

14. And indeed, the wicked will be in Hellfire.

15. They will [enter to] burn therein on the Day of Recompense,

16. And never therefrom will they be absent.

17. And what can make you know what is the Day of Recompense?

18. Then, what can make you know what is the Day of Recompense?

19. It is the Day when a soul will not possess for another soul [power to do] a thing; and the command, that Day, is [entirely] with Allah

سورة الإنفطار

Surat Al-Infiṭār | The Cleaving / The Splitting [82]

بِسْمِ اللَّهِ الرَّحْمَٰنِ الرَّحِيمِ

إِذَا السَّمَاءُ انفَطَرَتْ ﴿١﴾ وَإِذَا الْكَوَاكِبُ انتَثَرَتْ ﴿٢﴾ وَإِذَا الْبِحَارُ فُجِّرَتْ ﴿٣﴾ وَإِذَا الْقُبُورُ بُعْثِرَتْ ﴿٤﴾ عَلِمَتْ نَفْسٌ مَّا قَدَّمَتْ وَأَخَّرَتْ ﴿٥﴾ يَا أَيُّهَا الْإِنسَانُ مَا غَرَّكَ بِرَبِّكَ الْكَرِيمِ ﴿٦﴾ الَّذِي خَلَقَكَ فَسَوَّاكَ فَعَدَلَكَ ﴿٧﴾ فِي أَيِّ صُورَةٍ مَّا شَاءَ رَكَّبَكَ ﴿٨﴾ كَلَّا بَلْ تُكَذِّبُونَ بِالدِّينِ ﴿٩﴾ وَإِنَّ عَلَيْكُمْ لَحَافِظِينَ ﴿١٠﴾ كِرَامًا كَاتِبِينَ ﴿١١﴾ يَعْلَمُونَ مَا تَفْعَلُونَ ﴿١٢﴾ إِنَّ الْأَبْرَارَ لَفِي نَعِيمٍ ﴿١٣﴾ وَإِنَّ الْفُجَّارَ لَفِي جَحِيمٍ ﴿١٤﴾ يَصْلَوْنَهَا يَوْمَ الدِّينِ ﴿١٥﴾ وَمَا هُمْ عَنْهَا بِغَائِبِينَ ﴿١٦﴾ وَمَا أَدْرَاكَ مَا يَوْمُ الدِّينِ ﴿١٧﴾ ثُمَّ مَا أَدْرَاكَ مَا يَوْمُ الدِّينِ ﴿١٨﴾ يَوْمَ لَا تَمْلِكُ نَفْسٌ لِّنَفْسٍ شَيْئًا وَالْأَمْرُ يَوْمَئِذٍ لِّلَّهِ ﴿١٩﴾

1. When the sun is wrapped up [in darkness]

2. And when the stars fall, dispersing,

3. And when the mountains are removed

4. And when full-term she-camels are neglected

5. And when the wild beasts are gathered

6. And when the seas are filled with flame

7. And when the souls are paired

8. And when the girl [who was] buried alive is asked

9. For what sin she was killed

10. And when the pages are made public

11. And when the sky is stripped away

12. And when Hellfire is set ablaze

13. And when Paradise is brought near,

14. A soul will [then] know what it has brought [with it].

15. So I swear by the retreating stars –

16. Those that run [their courses] and disappear –

17. And by the night as it closes in

18. And by the dawn when it breathes

بِسْمِ اللَّهِ الرَّحْمَٰنِ الرَّحِيمِ

إِذَا الشَّمْسُ كُوِّرَتْ ﴿١﴾ وَإِذَا النُّجُومُ انكَدَرَتْ ﴿٢﴾ وَإِذَا الْجِبَالُ سُيِّرَتْ ﴿٣﴾ وَإِذَا الْعِشَارُ عُطِّلَتْ ﴿٤﴾ وَإِذَا الْوُحُوشُ حُشِرَتْ ﴿٥﴾ وَإِذَا الْبِحَارُ سُجِّرَتْ ﴿٦﴾ وَإِذَا النُّفُوسُ زُوِّجَتْ ﴿٧﴾ وَإِذَا الْمَوْءُودَةُ سُئِلَتْ ﴿٨﴾ بِأَيِّ ذَنبٍ قُتِلَتْ ﴿٩﴾ وَإِذَا الصُّحُفُ نُشِرَتْ ﴿١٠﴾ وَإِذَا السَّمَاءُ كُشِطَتْ ﴿١١﴾ وَإِذَا الْجَحِيمُ سُعِّرَتْ ﴿١٢﴾ وَإِذَا الْجَنَّةُ أُزْلِفَتْ ﴿١٣﴾ عَلِمَتْ نَفْسٌ مَّا أَحْضَرَتْ ﴿١٤﴾ فَلَا أُقْسِمُ بِالْخُنَّسِ ﴿١٥﴾ الْجَوَارِ الْكُنَّسِ ﴿١٦﴾ وَاللَّيْلِ إِذَا عَسْعَسَ ﴿١٧﴾ وَالصُّبْحِ إِذَا تَنَفَّسَ ﴿١٨﴾

19. [That] indeed, it is a word [conveyed by] a noble messenger

20. [Who is] possessed of power and with the Owner of the Throne, secure [in position],

21. Obeyed there [in the heavens] and trustworthy.

22. And your companion is not [at all] mad.

23. And he has already seen him in the clear horizon.

24. And he is not a withholder of [knowledge of] the unseen.

25. And it is not the word of a devil, expelled [from the heavens].

26. So where are you going?

27. It is not except a reminder to the worlds

28. For whoever wills among you to take a right course.

29. And you do not will except that Allah wills – Lord of the worlds.

إِنَّهُ لَقَوْلُ رَسُولٍ كَرِيمٍ ﴿١٩﴾ ذِى قُوَّةٍ عِندَ ذِى ٱلْعَرْشِ مَكِينٍ ﴿٢٠﴾ مُّطَاعٍ ثَمَّ أَمِينٍ ﴿٢١﴾ وَمَا صَاحِبُكُم بِمَجْنُونٍ ﴿٢٢﴾ وَلَقَدْ رَءَاهُ بِٱلْأُفُقِ ٱلْمُبِينِ ﴿٢٣﴾ وَمَا هُوَ عَلَى ٱلْغَيْبِ بِضَنِينٍ ﴿٢٤﴾ وَمَا هُوَ بِقَوْلِ شَيْطَٰنٍ رَّجِيمٍ ﴿٢٥﴾ فَأَيْنَ تَذْهَبُونَ ﴿٢٦﴾ إِنْ هُوَ إِلَّا ذِكْرٌ لِّلْعَٰلَمِينَ ﴿٢٧﴾ لِمَن شَآءَ مِنكُمْ أَن يَسْتَقِيمَ ﴿٢٨﴾ وَمَا تَشَآءُونَ إِلَّا أَن يَشَآءَ ٱللَّهُ رَبُّ ٱلْعَٰلَمِينَ ﴿٢٩﴾

1. He frowned and turned away

2. Because there came to him the blind man, [interrupting].

3. But what would make you perceive, [O Muhammad], that perhaps he might be purified

4. Or be reminded and the remembrance would benefit him?

5. As for he who thinks himself without need,

6. To him you give attention.

7. And not upon you [is any blame] if he will not be purified.

8. But as for he who came to you striving [for knowledge]

9. While he fears [Allah],

10. From him you are distracted.

11. No! Indeed, these verses are a reminder;

12. So whoever wills may remember it.

13. [It is recorded] in honoured sheets,

14. Exalted and purified,

15. [Carried] by the hands of messenger-angels,

16. Noble and dutiful.

17. Cursed is man; how disbelieving is he.

18. From what thing did He create him?

19. From a sperm-drop He created him and destined for him;

20. Then He eased the way for him;

21. Then He causes his death and provides a grave for him.

22. Then when He wills, He will resurrect him.

23. No! Man has not yet accomplished what He commanded him.

24. Then let mankind look at his food

سورة عبس

Surāt ʿAbasa | He Frowned [80]

بِسْمِ اللَّهِ الرَّحْمَٰنِ الرَّحِيمِ

عَبَسَ وَتَوَلَّىٰ ﴿١﴾ أَن جَاءَهُ الْأَعْمَىٰ ﴿٢﴾ وَمَا يُدْرِيكَ لَعَلَّهُ يَزَّكَّىٰ ﴿٣﴾ أَوْ يَذَّكَّرُ فَتَنفَعَهُ الذِّكْرَىٰ ﴿٤﴾ أَمَّا مَنِ اسْتَغْنَىٰ ﴿٥﴾ فَأَنتَ لَهُ تَصَدَّىٰ ﴿٦﴾ وَمَا عَلَيْكَ أَلَّا يَزَّكَّىٰ ﴿٧﴾ وَأَمَّا مَن جَاءَكَ يَسْعَىٰ ﴿٨﴾ وَهُوَ يَخْشَىٰ ﴿٩﴾ فَأَنتَ عَنْهُ تَلَهَّىٰ ﴿١٠﴾ كَلَّا إِنَّهَا تَذْكِرَةٌ ﴿١١﴾ فَمَن شَاءَ ذَكَرَهُ ﴿١٢﴾ فِي صُحُفٍ مُّكَرَّمَةٍ ﴿١٣﴾ مَّرْفُوعَةٍ مُّطَهَّرَةٍ ﴿١٤﴾ بِأَيْدِي سَفَرَةٍ ﴿١٥﴾ كِرَامٍ بَرَرَةٍ ﴿١٦﴾ قُتِلَ الْإِنسَانُ مَا أَكْفَرَهُ ﴿١٧﴾ مِنْ أَيِّ شَيْءٍ خَلَقَهُ ﴿١٨﴾ مِن نُّطْفَةٍ خَلَقَهُ فَقَدَّرَهُ ﴿١٩﴾ ثُمَّ السَّبِيلَ يَسَّرَهُ ﴿٢٠﴾ ثُمَّ أَمَاتَهُ فَأَقْبَرَهُ ﴿٢١﴾ ثُمَّ إِذَا شَاءَ أَنشَرَهُ ﴿٢٢﴾ كَلَّا لَمَّا يَقْضِ مَا أَمَرَهُ ﴿٢٣﴾ فَلْيَنظُرِ الْإِنسَانُ إِلَىٰ طَعَامِهِ

25. How We poured down water in torrents,

26. Then We broke open the earth, splitting [it with sprouts],

27. And caused to grow within it grain

28. And grapes and herbage

29. And olive and palm trees

30. And gardens of dense shrubbery

31. And fruit and grass –

32. [As] enjoyment for you and your grazing livestock.

33. But when there comes the Deafening Blast

34. On the Day a man will flee from his brother

35. And his mother and his father

36. And his wife and his children,

37. For every man, that Day, will be a matter adequate for him.

38. [Some] faces, that Day, will be bright –

39. Laughing, rejoicing at good news.

40. And [other] faces, that Day, will have upon them dust.

41. Blackness will cover them.

42. Those are the disbelievers, the wicked ones.

سورة عبس

Surāt ʿAbasa | He Frowned [80] | Part 2

أَنَّا صَبَبْنَا الْمَاءَ صَبًّا ۝ ثُمَّ شَقَقْنَا الْأَرْضَ شَقًّا ۝ فَأَنْبَتْنَا فِيهَا حَبًّا ۝ وَعِنَبًا وَقَضْبًا ۝ وَزَيْتُونًا وَنَخْلًا ۝ وَحَدَائِقَ غُلْبًا ۝ وَفَاكِهَةً وَأَبًّا ۝ مَتَاعًا لَكُمْ وَلِأَنْعَامِكُمْ ۝ فَإِذَا جَاءَتِ الصَّاخَّةُ ۝ يَوْمَ يَفِرُّ الْمَرْءُ مِنْ أَخِيهِ ۝ وَأُمِّهِ وَأَبِيهِ ۝ وَصَاحِبَتِهِ وَبَنِيهِ ۝ لِكُلِّ امْرِئٍ مِنْهُمْ يَوْمَئِذٍ شَأْنٌ يُغْنِيهِ ۝ وُجُوهٌ يَوْمَئِذٍ مُسْفِرَةٌ ۝ ضَاحِكَةٌ مُسْتَبْشِرَةٌ ۝ وَوُجُوهٌ يَوْمَئِذٍ عَلَيْهَا غَبَرَةٌ ۝ تَرْهَقُهَا قَتَرَةٌ ۝ أُولَئِكَ هُمُ الْكَفَرَةُ الْفَجَرَةُ ۝

1. By those [angels] who extract with violence

2. And [by] those who remove with ease

3. And [by] those who glide [as if] swimming

4. And those who race each other in a race

5. And those who arrange [each] matter,

6. On the Day the blast [of the Horn] will convulse [creation],

7. There will follow it the subsequent [one].

8. Hearts, that Day, will tremble.

9. Their eyes humbled.

10. They are [presently] saying, "Will we indeed be returned to [our] former state [of life]?

11. Even if we should be decayed bones?"

12. They say, "That, then, would be a losing return."

13. Indeed, it will be but one shout,

14. And suddenly they will be [alert] upon the earth's surface.

15. Has there reached you the story of Moses –

16. When his Lord called to him in the sacred valley of Tuwa,

17. "Go to Pharaoh. Indeed, he has transgressed.

18. And say to him, 'Would you [be willing to] purify yourself

19. And let me guide you to your Lord so you would fear [Him]?'"

20. And he showed him the greatest sign,

21. But Pharaoh denied and disobeyed.

22. Then he turned his back, striving.

23. And he gathered [his people] and called out

24. And said, "I am your most exalted lord."

25. So Allah seized him in exemplary punishment for the last and the first [transgression].

26. Indeed in that is a lesson for whoever would fear [Allah].

سُورَةُ النَّازِعَاتِ

Surāt An-Nāzi'āt | Those Who Drag Forth [79]

بِسْمِ اللَّهِ الرَّحْمَٰنِ الرَّحِيمِ

وَالنَّازِعَاتِ غَرْقًا ﴿١﴾ وَالنَّاشِطَاتِ نَشْطًا ﴿٢﴾ وَالسَّابِحَاتِ سَبْحًا ﴿٣﴾ فَالسَّابِقَاتِ سَبْقًا ﴿٤﴾ فَالْمُدَبِّرَاتِ أَمْرًا ﴿٥﴾ يَوْمَ تَرْجُفُ الرَّاجِفَةُ ﴿٦﴾ تَتْبَعُهَا الرَّادِفَةُ ﴿٧﴾ قُلُوبٌ يَوْمَئِذٍ وَاجِفَةٌ ﴿٨﴾ أَبْصَارُهَا خَاشِعَةٌ ﴿٩﴾ يَقُولُونَ أَئِنَّا لَمَرْدُودُونَ فِي الْحَافِرَةِ ﴿١٠﴾ أَئِذَا كُنَّا عِظَامًا نَّخِرَةً ﴿١١﴾ قَالُوا تِلْكَ إِذًا كَرَّةٌ خَاسِرَةٌ ﴿١٢﴾ فَإِنَّمَا هِيَ زَجْرَةٌ وَاحِدَةٌ ﴿١٣﴾ فَإِذَا هُم بِالسَّاهِرَةِ ﴿١٤﴾ هَلْ أَتَاكَ حَدِيثُ مُوسَىٰ ﴿١٥﴾ إِذْ نَادَاهُ رَبُّهُ بِالْوَادِ الْمُقَدَّسِ طُوًى ﴿١٦﴾ اذْهَبْ إِلَىٰ فِرْعَوْنَ إِنَّهُ طَغَىٰ ﴿١٧﴾ فَقُلْ هَل لَّكَ إِلَىٰ أَن تَزَكَّىٰ ﴿١٨﴾ وَأَهْدِيَكَ إِلَىٰ رَبِّكَ فَتَخْشَىٰ ﴿١٩﴾ فَأَرَاهُ الْآيَةَ الْكُبْرَىٰ ﴿٢٠﴾ فَكَذَّبَ وَعَصَىٰ ﴿٢١﴾ ثُمَّ أَدْبَرَ يَسْعَىٰ ﴿٢٢﴾ فَحَشَرَ فَنَادَىٰ ﴿٢٣﴾ فَقَالَ أَنَا رَبُّكُمُ الْأَعْلَىٰ ﴿٢٤﴾ فَأَخَذَهُ اللَّهُ نَكَالَ الْآخِرَةِ وَالْأُولَىٰ ﴿٢٥﴾ إِنَّ فِي ذَٰلِكَ لَعِبْرَةً لِّمَن يَخْشَىٰ ﴿٢٦﴾

27. Are you a more difficult creation or is the heaven? Allah constructed it.

28. He raised its ceiling and proportioned it.

29. And He darkened its night and extracted its brightness.

30. And after that He spread the earth.

31. He extracted from it its water and its pasture,

32. And the mountains He set firmly

33. As provision for you and your grazing livestock.

34. But when there comes the greatest Overwhelming Calamity –

35. The Day when man will remember that for which he strove,

36. And Hellfire will be exposed for [all] those who see –

37. So as for he who transgressed

38. And preferred the life of the world,

39. Then indeed, Hellfire will be [his] refuge.

40. But as for he who feared the position of his Lord and prevented the soul from [unlawful] inclination,

41. Then indeed, Paradise will be [his] refuge.

42. They ask you, [O Muhammad], about the Hour: when is its arrival?

43. In what [position] are you that you should mention it?

44. To your Lord is its finality.

45. You are only a warner for those who fear it.

46. It will be, on the Day they see it, as though they had not remained [in the world] except for an afternoon or a morning thereof.

ءَأَنتُمْ أَشَدُّ خَلْقًا أَمِ السَّمَاءُ بَنَاهَا ﴿٢٧﴾ رَفَعَ سَمْكَهَا فَسَوَّىٰهَا ﴿٢٨﴾

وَأَغْطَشَ لَيْلَهَا وَأَخْرَجَ ضُحَاهَا ﴿٢٩﴾ وَالْأَرْضَ بَعْدَ ذَٰلِكَ دَحَاهَا ﴿٣٠﴾

أَخْرَجَ مِنْهَا مَاءَهَا وَمَرْعَاهَا ﴿٣١﴾ وَالْجِبَالَ أَرْسَاهَا ﴿٣٢﴾ مَتَاعًا لَّكُمْ

وَلِأَنْعَامِكُمْ ﴿٣٣﴾ فَإِذَا جَاءَتِ الطَّامَّةُ الْكُبْرَىٰ ﴿٣٤﴾ يَوْمَ يَتَذَكَّرُ الْإِنسَانُ

مَا سَعَىٰ ﴿٣٥﴾ وَبُرِّزَتِ الْجَحِيمُ لِمَن يَرَىٰ ﴿٣٦﴾ فَأَمَّا مَن طَغَىٰ ﴿٣٧﴾ وَآثَرَ

الْحَيَاةَ الدُّنْيَا ﴿٣٨﴾ فَإِنَّ الْجَحِيمَ هِيَ الْمَأْوَىٰ ﴿٣٩﴾ وَأَمَّا مَنْ خَافَ

مَقَامَ رَبِّهِ وَنَهَى النَّفْسَ عَنِ الْهَوَىٰ ﴿٤٠﴾ فَإِنَّ الْجَنَّةَ هِيَ الْمَأْوَىٰ

﴿٤١﴾ يَسْأَلُونَكَ عَنِ السَّاعَةِ أَيَّانَ مُرْسَاهَا ﴿٤٢﴾ فِيمَ أَنتَ مِن

ذِكْرَاهَا ﴿٤٣﴾ إِلَىٰ رَبِّكَ مُنتَهَاهَا ﴿٤٤﴾ إِنَّمَا أَنتَ مُنذِرُ مَن يَخْشَاهَا

﴿٤٥﴾ كَأَنَّهُمْ يَوْمَ يَرَوْنَهَا لَمْ يَلْبَثُوا إِلَّا عَشِيَّةً أَوْ ضُحَاهَا ﴿٤٦﴾

1. About what are they asking one another?

2. About the great news -

3. That over which they are in disagreement.

4. No! They are going to know.

5. Then, no! They are going to know.

6. Have We not made the earth a resting place?

7. And the mountains as stakes?

8. And We created you in pairs

9. And made your sleep [a means for] rest

10. And made the night as clothing

11. And made the day for livelihood

12. And constructed above you seven strong [heavens]

13. And made the sun as a shining lamp?

14. And sent down, from the rain clouds, pouring water

15. That We may bring forth thereby grain and vegetation

16. And gardens of entwined growth.

17. Indeed, the Day of Judgement is an appointed time -

18. The Day the Horn is blown and you will come forth in multitudes

19. And the heaven is opened and will become gateways

20. And the mountains are removed and will be [but] a mirage.

21. Indeed, Hell has been lying in wait -

22. For the transgressors, a place of return,

23. In which they will remain for ages [unending]

24. They will not taste therein [any] coolness or drink

سورة النبأ

Surāt An-Naba' | The Tidings / The Announcement [78]

بِسْمِ اللَّهِ الرَّحْمَٰنِ الرَّحِيمِ

عَمَّ يَتَسَاءَلُونَ ۝ عَنِ النَّبَإِ الْعَظِيمِ ۝ الَّذِي هُمْ فِيهِ مُخْتَلِفُونَ ۝

كَلَّا سَيَعْلَمُونَ ۝ ثُمَّ كَلَّا سَيَعْلَمُونَ ۝ أَلَمْ نَجْعَلِ الْأَرْضَ مِهَادًا ۝

وَالْجِبَالَ أَوْتَادًا ۝ وَخَلَقْنَاكُمْ أَزْوَاجًا ۝ وَجَعَلْنَا نَوْمَكُمْ سُبَاتًا

۝ وَجَعَلْنَا اللَّيْلَ لِبَاسًا ۝ وَجَعَلْنَا النَّهَارَ مَعَاشًا ۝ وَبَنَيْنَا

فَوْقَكُمْ سَبْعًا شِدَادًا ۝ وَجَعَلْنَا سِرَاجًا وَهَّاجًا ۝ وَأَنْزَلْنَا مِنَ

الْمُعْصِرَاتِ مَاءً ثَجَّاجًا ۝ لِنُخْرِجَ بِهِ حَبًّا وَنَبَاتًا ۝ وَجَنَّاتٍ

أَلْفَافًا ۝ إِنَّ يَوْمَ الْفَصْلِ كَانَ مِيقَاتًا ۝ يَوْمَ يُنْفَخُ فِي الصُّورِ

فَتَأْتُونَ أَفْوَاجًا ۝ وَفُتِحَتِ السَّمَاءُ فَكَانَتْ أَبْوَابًا ۝ وَسُيِّرَتِ

الْجِبَالُ فَكَانَتْ سَرَابًا ۝ إِنَّ جَهَنَّمَ كَانَتْ مِرْصَادًا ۝ لِلطَّاغِينَ

مَآبًا ۝ لَابِثِينَ فِيهَا أَحْقَابًا ۝ لَا يَذُوقُونَ فِيهَا بَرْدًا وَلَا شَرَابًا

95

25. Except scalding water and [foul] purulence –

26. An appropriate recompense.

27. Indeed, they were not expecting an account

28. And denied Our verses with [emphatic] denial.

29. But all things We have enumerated in writing.

30. So taste [the penalty], and never will We increase you except in torment.

31. Indeed, for the righteous is attainment –

32. Gardens and grapevines

33. And full-breasted [companions] of equal age

34. And a full cup.

35. No ill speech will they hear therein or any falsehood –

36. [As] reward from your Lord, [a generous] gift [made due by] account,

37. [From] the Lord of the heavens and the earth and whatever is between them, the Most Merciful.

38. Indeed, He who created them is, for their sake, Knowing.

39. And indeed, the righteous will be in pleasure,

40. On adorned couches, observing.

إِلَّا حَمِيمًا وَغَسَّاقًا ﴿٢٥﴾ جَزَاءً وِفَاقًا ﴿٢٦﴾ إِنَّهُمْ كَانُوا لَا يَرْجُونَ حِسَابًا ﴿٢٧﴾ وَكَذَّبُوا بِآيَاتِنَا كِذَّابًا ﴿٢٨﴾ وَكُلَّ شَيْءٍ أَحْصَيْنَاهُ كِتَابًا ﴿٢٩﴾ فَذُوقُوا فَلَن نَّزِيدَكُمْ إِلَّا عَذَابًا ﴿٣٠﴾ إِنَّ لِلْمُتَّقِينَ مَفَازًا ﴿٣١﴾ حَدَائِقَ وَأَعْنَابًا ﴿٣٢﴾ وَكَوَاعِبَ أَتْرَابًا ﴿٣٣﴾ وَكَأْسًا دِهَاقًا ﴿٣٤﴾ لَّا يَسْمَعُونَ فِيهَا لَغْوًا وَلَا كِذَّابًا ﴿٣٥﴾ جَزَاءً مِّن رَّبِّكَ عَطَاءً حِسَابًا ﴿٣٦﴾ رَّبِّ السَّمَاوَاتِ وَالْأَرْضِ وَمَا بَيْنَهُمَا الرَّحْمَٰنِ لَا يَمْلِكُونَ مِنْهُ خِطَابًا ﴿٣٧﴾ يَوْمَ يَقُومُ الرُّوحُ وَالْمَلَائِكَةُ صَفًّا لَّا يَتَكَلَّمُونَ إِلَّا مَنْ أَذِنَ لَهُ الرَّحْمَٰنُ وَقَالَ صَوَابًا ﴿٢٨﴾ ذَٰلِكَ الْيَوْمُ الْحَقُّ فَمَن شَاءَ اتَّخَذَ إِلَىٰ رَبِّهِ مَآبًا ﴿٣٩﴾ إِنَّا أَنذَرْنَاكُمْ عَذَابًا قَرِيبًا يَوْمَ يَنظُرُ الْمَرْءُ مَا قَدَّمَتْ يَدَاهُ وَيَقُولُ الْكَافِرُ يَا لَيْتَنِي كُنتُ تُرَابًا ﴿٤٠﴾

Dedicated to

My wonderful boys Taha and Yasin, who both make me the proudest father, and to my beautiful wife, Shabana, to whom every book I write is dedicated, unconditionally!

Acknowledgments

I would like to express my gratitude to all my students at the University of Edinburgh, for their generous and valuable suggestions, corrections, support and encouragement in this venture. Any shortcomings remaining in the book are my responsibility.

Final Words

I hope you enjoyed using this reader and found it helpful. I would love to hear from you and your personal experience of how you are benefiting from this book. If you have any questions, please feel free to get in touch via m.diouri@me.com , Twitter: @e_Arabic or at mouradd.com

Mourad Diouri

Edinburgh, Scotland

2 Jul 2025

Browse our full catalogue at

MosaicTree.org

Arabic Script & Sounds

Arabic Vocabulary

Arabic for Little Ones

Arabic/Islamic Mosaic &
Calligraphy

Arabic Learning Journals

Well-Being & Character
Development

Mosaic Tree Press

MosaicTree.org

بحمد الله تم

Completed with Praise & Thanks to God